What Price Religion?

What Price Religion?

Christoph Türcke

SCM PRESS LTD

Translated by John Bowden from the German
*Religionswende. Eine Dogmatik in
Bruchstücken*, published 1995 by Dietrich zu
Klampen Verlag, Lüneburg

0 334 02688 1

First published 1997 by
SCM Press Ltd
9–17 St Albans Place London N1 0NX

Typeset by Regent Typesetting, London

Printed in Great Britain by
Biddles Ltd, Guildford and King's Lynn

Contents

Foreword

'The criticism of religion is the presupposition of all criticism' was a much-quoted formula at the end of the 1960s. At that time of student movements in the industrialized countries atheism was regarded as the spice of active social criticism. Today avowed atheists seem like a survival of a past era. Why? Has modern science meanwhile discovered what theology can merely conjure up, the actual existence of a higher being who bears the sins of the world or guarantees its meaning in some other way? Not at all. Science cannot even establish whether the world is eternal or has a beginning (the Big Bang is only a relative beginning), far less provide for a good end; the most highly developed medicine can still only put off death, and a 'kind' end is only a relatively good one. So no science will ever silence the religious need. But none of its voids indicates that there is something to fill them, and to stop them up with certainties of faith ('*God* is the absolute beginning, and he ensures a good *end*') is the most dishonest way of making theological capital out of them. An architect who built on such an uncertain foundation as religion has done would belong in prison.

No, atheism has not been refuted; history has simply

passed it by. In the nineteenth century, with the industrialization of Europe, it became a mass phenomenon. Since industrialization is no longer automatically associated with the expectation of a better human future, and the possibility of socialism has largely faded, atheism has lost a decisive support. The religious renaissance which has come about in the last quarter of a century could only have escaped the notice of those who measure religious practice by church attendance in Central Europe and numbers of church members. These have of course gone down. But those who can no longer believe in the Christian God have kept a soft spot for UFOs, cosmic energies and other higher beings. According to recent surveys, almost every one of them still feels 'somehow religious', even if they do not have words to express it. And once we look beyond the rim of Europe to the Middle East, to Africa, India, South America, the advance of religious forces is unmistakable.

There are plenty of analyses of this development. They register the growth of so-called fundamentalism and interpret it as a flight from modernity or its expression; they see either the true nature of human beings or the influence of society at work in the persistence of religion, which they regret or welcome – and treat the decisive factor, the *content* of religion, like a hot potato. Where it is not their own religion, the fear of burning their mouth on it can be seen everywhere in public discussion: clearly there is a tendency to let it rest as long as it moves within the realm of legality, or to describe it in courteous, neutral terms. This is certainly a good start in an age when religious hatreds are flaring up again: not to pass judgment immediately, but first of all to describe, to gain some understanding of the thought and the cultural background behind convictions which are not one's own. However, if that is as far as things go and people cease to ask whether there is any indubitably true content to religion, or whether all religions, however different they may be in level and origin, are not united by some kind of secret agreement to lead people to believe in the existence of some higher being and some higher forces which create meaning, then tolerance towards those of other views turns into a kind of cunning cultural relativism. Its basic method is: 'I respect your message and you respect mine, and let's allow the market to decide who wins.' This relativism assumes the role of a divine judgment which is not expressed by the victor in a duel or on the field of honour, but by the better marketing of one side.

Anyone who, like Max Weber, regards religious convictions as a realm of subjective values in which there is no truth or untruth, wheat or chaff, according to any kind of scientific judgment, but only a personal preference for this or that, has not only insulated any religious content from criticism but has subjected all religion uncritically to the laws of the market. The divine judgment of these laws is usually milder than that of the military or the Inquisition, but no less dogmatic: the one who wins the contest is right. Thus modern religious relativism is merely the counterpart of the old dogmatism: what doctrine was for the latter, the market is for the former, and what neither of them wants to hear is the question of truth.

Any account of religious rites among the Amazon

Indians today finds a public; any advertising for a sect some following; any Catholic dissident some media interest. But in the age of commercial broadcasting, who will explain whether these rites and this advertising are not perhaps the simple, crude form of a pretence about something which does not exist? And is not the same thing happening at the level of theological discussion between dissidents and the church's magisterium, but in a rather more subtle way, namely, washed with all the waters of the Enlightenment? In fact the religious groups are no different from all the other associations and parties. They have become commercial stations for their own messages, and the collapse of the audience which investigates these messages seriously can hardly be studied better than in noting the disproportion between the advance of religion all over society and the disappearance of any public critical discussion of it.

To discuss these issues is the purpose of this book, which has grown out of a series of articles in *Die Zeit*. By way of example I have taken ten terms which not only have a manifestly religious character but continue to survive in everyday terminology. Those who think that they can use them in an open or neutral way, or devoid of religious intent, do not know what they are doing.

Blasphemy

Christ on the cross with gas mask and army boots; the cross beam broken off at both ends; Christ's left hand, which this releases, holding high a little cross; the whole picture signed 'keep your mouth shut and go on serving': this little drawing of 1928 involved George Grosz in a famous blasphemy (= contempt for religion) case in 1928. He got off lightly, but the question remained: was this contempt or just a description?

For an answer, one has only to leaf through the theology of the First World War in documents in which the biblical saying 'But he who perseveres to the end will be saved' (Matt. 10.22) is interpreted to mean: 'Christianity is now wartime service in which even the sacrifice of one's life may not be refused. Christ has come to drive Satan, "the prince of this world", out of his kingdom.' 'Death on the battlefield can enjoy … the whole praise and merit of a martyr.' 'The brave man must stand at his post and hold out.' Thus the Jesuit Christian Pesch in 1915;[1] he could also have been a Protestant. The war theology of that time was ecumenical and international, unanimous that the Christian nations of the West were stirring people up to reciprocal mass slaughter in the name of the God whom they all claimed to worship.

What Price Religion?

Grosz's controversial drawing is a seismograph of the First World War. *That* had given Christ a gas mask and army boots; he, Grosz, had merely depicted the atrocity. The fact that Christ is stretching out a little cross into the void, as if he wanted to conjure up the invisible from there to take the mask off him, restores to the large cross something of its authenticity as an instrument of torture and execution which it had long lost as a symbol standing on the altar or as a ceremonial sign made by the clergy. The real cross is a shock: tortured humanity as the picture puzzle of a God who should put an end to all torture – and does not come. Reduced to a symbol, the trade mark of a prosperous religious move-ment, the cross gives another message: 'In this sign you will conquer'. Tortured humankind now shines out as God's will, as haloes would later shine out around the heads of saints. With the simplest means Grosz depicts the scandalous shift of values which the scandal of the cross of Christ underwent in Christianity. The gas mask is a hallmark of the First World War and a piece of equipment which no longer allows the crucified one even to cry out his 'My God, my God, why have you forsaken me' (Matt. 27.46). This is replaced by the laconic inscription underneath, 'Keep your mouth shut and go on serving': that is the twentieth-century theo-logy of the cross, not blasphemy.

And what if nevertheless many of our contemporaries can see nothing in it but a manifest insult to their religious feelings? That shows what a dark chapter religious feelings are. They do not fall from heaven pure and simple, but are formed in a lengthy development. It is a long way from the first terror or shudder that someone feels at natural events which threaten him or transcend his comprehension to the fixing of supernatural authorities who are permanently revered as the founders of order and meaning, as lawgivers, judges and saviours. On that way the spiritual disposition of a collective is gradually orientated and moved in such a direction that it finally finds particular rituals, cultic practices and beliefs as natural as though they had been sung at the cradle of all humankind and were not the product of centuries of internal and external disciplining.

While it is certain that a human being to whom nothing is holy is a rough, unscrupulous being, it has to be said that scruples, awe, reverence for something higher, are not in themselves an indication of tenderness and humanity. Initially they were nothing but means of self-assertion, imposed by an impenetrable, overpowering, threatening nature which one had to try to please with bloody sacrificial victims, so as not to fall victim to it oneself. Need and violence are the residue of religious feelings, and there is no lack of them where this feeling leads from a fluttering, diffuse stirring to a firmly defined cult, or is even developed into a whole culture. How did Christianity arrive at a point when eventually believers simply could not help genuflecting before the altar, making the sign of the cross at the mention of the Holy Trinity or the Mother of God, and receiving the host with a shudder of reverence? Solely through friendly persuasion? Was it not also at least because the most fearful example was made of those who did not want to engage in such physical reactions? Even if many believers today no longer regard the Inquisition as true

Christianity, its contribution to the internalization of that faith which no longer wants to remember it is incalculable. The visual lesson provided by the smoking pyres on which heretics were burned was just as much a part of the preparation of the soul as edifying preaching and acts of charity.

Furthermore, blasphemy is contempt for religion, but no religion triumphs without becoming blasphemous. Of course it was an insult to the feelings of all Muslims when Pope Innocent III called Muhammad the 'Beast of the Apocalypse' and the Christian crusaders relieved themselves in mosques. Of course it was a violation of the religious feelings of all Jews when Luther suggested that instead of Holy Scripture they should read that 'Bible which is under the pig's tail, and gobble up the letters that fall from it'.[2] And of course similar attacks can be demonstrated in Judaism and Islam. So blasphemy has not been invented in modern times, but simply been given a new nuance: to contempt for other religions has been added contempt for religion as such. Writings about the 'Three Deceivers', namely Moses, Jesus and Muhammad, were secretly going the rounds in the seventeenth century, and finally, at the beginning of the eighteenth, a French country priest called Jean Meslier, who all his life had read mass in his village like a good *curé*, went so far in his testament as to deny the existence of *any* higher being. For him religion was even the superstition from which it pretended to bring deliverance. Though Christianity might seem to be its highest stage of development, to anyone who had sound common sense or simply observed the principle that contradictions are to be avoided in stories like these,

4

which stated that all at once evil sprang out of a world which was created thoroughly good or that the whole of humankind was to be cast into hell for a bit of fruit stolen from a hidden tree, it was clear how ridiculous it was to revere the Bible as the embodiment of all truth.[3]

Since then blasphemy has taken on the appearance of a nihilistic spectre. Only someone to whom nothing is holy can really be a blasphemer. Blasphemy goes with a person's notion of anarchy, lack of respect for any values and principles, i.e. for any cultural achievements which religion has brought with it in the course of millennia. While scruples, awe, reverence for something higher are not in themselves a proof of humanity, there can be no humanity without them. Inhibitions about giving free rein to one's own lusts or one's own anger regardless of anything else stem first from fear of a higher authority which prohibits this. There are no norms which did not initially have a religious basis. Religion is the mother of all morality, however immorally it may have raged in history.

From that perspective the indignation of those who feel disappointed or deceived by it is only too under-standable, and the assertion that to the blasphemer nothing is holy is demagogy. It does not apply directly even to the Marquis of Sade, who could link the divine Trinity with every conceivable obscenity in the most virtuoso way. He preaches the cult of a rigorous maxi-mizing of pleasure, to which any religion, etiquette, custom, friendship, indeed any scruple, is to be sacri-ficed as superstition. Anything may be destroyed and mocked for the sake of the cult of pleasure, but he himself will tolerate no mockery – and that tendency is already the snag that puts paid to all pleasure. Moreover in the orgies of violence and sex in which Sade's principal characters engage, the ongoing incitement to enjoyment and pleasure declines, like reining oneself in to a final stop. 'O my friends, let us only have orgasm together: that is the only happiness of life,'[4] cries one of them in sexual ecstasy, which he thus indicates as the last way of deadening his sorrowfulness at death. Pleasure which has become an idol and is made compulsory soon gets stale, and its priest, Sade, is not so unlike his Christian opponents: his longing for unscrupulous enjoyment is the negative counterpart to the Christian longing for a bliss without any twinge of conscience. Moreover, the cynicism that he disarmingly displays here reveals and at the same time puts to shame the suppressed and the denied element which prevails where pleasure *before* death is attacked in the name of eternal pleasure and bliss *after* death. Sade is a radical anti-humanist – to the verge of being a representative of radically enlightened humanity. The extremes meet in his blasphemy.

No, don't worry: blasphemy is not simply the same thing as enlightenment. But sometimes enlightenment looks confusingly like blasphemy. When it hits the spot, mockery penetrates deeper than any other form of criticism. Sometimes a joke, a satire, a caricature succeeds where long arguments often fail, in showing how vain, how puffed-up, how arrogant authorities are. Mockery is cynical where it makes fun of the wretched. It enlightens wherever, in a flash, it brings out what is ridiculous, if need be distorting it until it becomes recognizable. Criticism without mockery is toothless: it does not really bite and is not meant completely seriously. Therefore if it was to be serious, the religious criticism of the Enlightenment could not help now and then insulting the religious authorities and the feelings they cherished. Sporadic mockery gave its attack an edge.

When Christianity was still great and strong and imposed itself on all members of society as the only way to salvation, contempt for religion meant resistance to the highest truth – and seemed so tremendously repre-hensible because it was completely unreasonable and self-destructive. By engaging in it, people cut themselves off from Christianity, indeed from the basic rules of everyday understanding. No one in their senses could want that. Meanwhile, in bourgeois society, which appeals to human rights, not to divine commandments, and declares religion to be a private matter, the act of blasphemy has been losing its contours. Its contempt is no longer for the truth, since it is no longer conceded that any kind of faith has the exclusive truth, but for any religious feelings as such which might lay claim to inviolability, regardless of their content. Because reli-gious feelings consist in regarding as holy something about which nothing more can be ascertained, the feelings themselves are regarded as holy – at any rate to the degree that Article 166 of the German penal code explicitly provides protection against 'maliciously reviling confessions, religious societies and ideological associations'. Even in a modern pluralistic society, which regards a person's attitude to religion as his or her own private affair, blasphemy is regarded as some-thing that can be objectified. However, the criterion for it is whether someone feels insulted, and is therefore purely subjective. This criterion draws no distinction between the humiliated and the offended, the offended party whose vanity has been hurt. And think how many odd things today are promoted by 'religious societies and ideological associations' as 'true', without the least concern for their compatibility with a highly techno-logical modern environment. Think how presumptuous religious feeling is in canvassing for support without the slightest respect for the idea of truth.

Enlightenment that is any use hurts; sometimes it cannot avoid insulting religious feelings by clearly pointing out their shamelessness. The blasphemy para-graph is opposed to it. It still smacks of the nihilistic spectre which went around in the early days of moder-nity, those free spirits to whom nothing seemed holy because they declared war on religion as such. The present practice of religion is certainly free, but, says the blasphemy law surreptitiously, better some religion than none at all; better reverence for something higher than reverence for nothing higher. It does not matter so much what principles one has, but one must have some principles to be socially compatible.

In contrast to blasphemy, the blasphemy law pro-vokes virtually no indignation. It corresponds to a col-lective semi-conscious and unconscious which through millennia of schooling has internalized terror at chaos and respect for the holy and the exalted to the verge of making it a conditioned reflex. To this degree modern society is anything but blasphemous. Any nonsense that it creates as a world-view in order to attract believers and draw on religious feelings enjoys its protection, as long as this does not attack its basic laws. In the realm of competing religious feelings, where opportunities are equal, none is to be disparaged. However, anyone who regarded as blasphemous, i.e. as a prostitution of the holy by its own representatives, this competitive situation, the so-called 'market of possibilities' in which the religious and confessional communities put themselves on offer and seek to polish up their image with expensive advertising campaigns, would not find a hearing in the courts. Virtually no one takes offence at *this* form of prostitution in a capitalistic society. It is the elixir of life for all those who have to offer their labour for sale. That there could be a gigantic blasphemy in the fact that the substance of religion can only prosper to the degree that it is packaged as a commodity and successfully sold is not even thought about. Anyone who called a church government which commissioned clever advertising agencies to launch statements of belief using the methods that succeed with computers and cars a procurement company for Christianity would appear before the courts for offensive behaviour, whereas the contempt for religion by which *he* felt offended is not even provided for in the blasphemy law.

The blasphemy law is modern, since it conforms with the market; it is archaic, since under the guise of religious neutrality it cultivates a deep-seated respect for a holy which is not further defined. And in both respects it goes against the Enlightenment: it protects beliefs which have every occasion to shun the light of reason, along with the ostentatious cult of commodities, which need not fear reason as long as it is the condition for its social life. But that is not all. Because the blasphemy law does not take into account just injured vanity but also the humiliated and insulted who incur mockery because they suffer hurt, although it is contrary to the Enlightenment, it can nevertheless hold up a mirror to the Enlightenment and make it reflect on its humane content.

Enlightenment cannot be serious without scorn and mockery. But scorn and mockery were always part of the Enlightenment only where they showed a way out of oppression, where the weak used them as a weapon against the powerful, who had less wit but stronger battalions. Of course scorn and mockery are still part of the final victory, but where they do not become irrelevant as a result of the victory, where they form the victor's cry of triumph, they are repulsive. When the Nazis showed contempt for the Jews, a stupid, racist resentment was being shown against a religion on whose intellectual achievements critical thought still draws on more than it usually realizes. When Europeans mock the ancestor cult of the Amazon Indians, they pride themselves on how far they have come and celebrate the victory of colonialism in the most stupid way. Moreover such victorious poses are not signs of enlightenment if what the victors claim to have pulled to pieces is really superstition. It is not even certain how enlightened it would be to tell the poor wretches in the favelas of Sao Paulo, Mexico or Recife how nonsensical was the Pentecostal religion to which they desperately cling, because they have nothing else but hunger and children. At all events there are situations in which the dignity of the wretched is respected more if one keeps quiet and recognizes that further enlightenment would amount to showing off by the privileged.

Blasphemy

Blasphemy is not meaningless in itself. It is concerned with specific issues: Who shows contempt for what religion and how? Who feels offended and why? Many of the Muslims who regard the death sentence passed by Ayatollah Khomeini on the writer Salman Rushdie as an unjustifiable monstrosity were nevertheless indignant at his novel *The Satanic Verses*. This was not simply out of sexual prudery, as Richard Webster has shown, but because they were stamped by the experience of 'centuries of Christian polemic and the statements of Western orientalists', who attributed to Islam 'a fantastic, disreputable or diabolical sexuality'. When Rushdie had prostitutes in a brothel called Hijab (the term for the veil which Muslim women have to wear) taking the names of the wives of Muhammad and slipping into their roles, even very moderate Muslims felt the oldest European denunciations coming alive again – through someone who had been brought up in Islam, who should have known better and nevertheless became a mouthpiece for the 'terrifying, triumphant hatred which the West has nurtured for Islam since its origins'.[5]

Dark Islamic fundamentalism versus Western democracy, freedom of speech and enlightenment: this scheme is truly too simple for the Rushdie case. Just as certainly as the indignation of offended vanity is not that of the humiliated and the hurt, so there are certainly borderline cases between the two which cannot be decided one way or the other. For example, it is by no means clear what kind of indignation caused the storm against Rushdie even *before* Khomeini pronounced his barbaric *fatwah* against him. And was Rushdie's deliberate sexual language enlightened wit or cheap triumphalism?

The question is not settled by his subsequent assurance that of course he had only the former in mind, even if, as doubtless may be supposed, he was being honest.

Natural though it is to plead for Rushdie's liberation, one thing must be learned urgently from his misfortune. Muslims predominantly from Europe have come to feel that the mockery which accompanies the Enlightenment investigation of the unproven, a category into which principles of faith now unavoidably fall, is an import, like all the other compulsory imports to which the West has introduced them. They never had the opportunity to come to know the liberating wit of the oppressed here, but from the start experienced it as a conspiracy with colonialism and inexorable modernization, as a malicious and frivolous adjunct to the economic and political victory which the West had won over the Islamic East. It was hard for them to distinguish between democracy and imperialism because they had never really *experienced* a distinction between the two, and this concrete experience weighs just as heavily as the abstract knowledge that the two *need* not necessarily mean the same thing. It is that which makes the situation so complicated – and Rushdie not simply a hero of freedom of speech.

There can be no double standards. Criticism which has proved correct against the lack of proof and rigidity of Christian principles of faith will not be wrong if it is applied to those of Islam. But enlightenment which wants to be more than just right must learn to assess where its mockery begins to take on the triumphalist tone which insults the humiliated more than it unmasks presumption – and where it would betray itself if it took account of such subtleties. That does not justify the dark sides of the blasphemy clauses, but it does show how little would be gained by their abolition: even their objection to the cynical triumph of the victors would fail.

Martyrdom

In German, the word for torture, *Marter*, is very close to that for martyrdom, but in fact the original Greek *martys*, from which 'martyrdom' is initially derived, means something different, namely 'witness'. The witness is the one who speaks up for the truth of a disputed matter before the court, confirms it, and if need be swears to it. He is neither defendant nor prosecutor, but in that he helps to condemn or acquit, he is not simply neutral either. And if what he is talking about is not merely an isolated fact – theft, robbery, murder, adultery – but a whole world-view which is difficult to present without declaring oneself for or against it, in the twinkling of an eye the witness can himself become the defendant. Anyone who is not afraid of bearing witness, is not deterred by any threat or any suffering from defending the world-view or *idea* which he firmly believes to be the truth, and is willing to give his life for it, is a witness in the highest sense of the word, a martyr.

'Martyr' is a title of honour. Even those who do not share the convictions for which martyrs suffer usually cannot help respecting them for their courage and commitment. And that respect therefore extends to their convictions. Can what someone has suffered torture or death for have been mere humbug? Doesn't the credibility of his self-sacrifice for his cause also make the cause itself credible? The fact that someone died for an idea does not change it, yet through that death the idea gains that much more power of conviction. It has a testimony on its side which throws more weight on to the scales and moves people in a different way from mere arguments. The idea is hallowed by its martyr, and he is hallowed by it. It is no accident that the legends of the Christian saints are predominantly stories of martyrs.

The notion of martyrdom contributes towards a tremendous revaluation of values: it interprets the downfall of the individual as the rise of his cause, and manifest personal defeat as victory at a level above the personal. Plato showed this in a classic way by means of the trial of Socrates. Accused of having despised the gods of Athens and led its youth astray, Socrates has to defend himself; in defending himself he cannot do other than take the charge apart point by point; in doing so he can only act as he always has done, dissecting the supposed wisdom and virtue of his fellow citizens with deliberate questions in such a way that they no longer know where they are. He sees himself compelled to use the very proceedings that they have brought against him and the charge that has been laid against him, but by refuting the charge so devastatingly he confirms the motives of his accusers, stirs up their wrath and provokes their destruction. So he perishes *by* his reason and *for* it. But through his sacrifice to it as an individual, this reason achieves the most splendid triumph, as he does in it. He becomes immortal in the memory of his friends and pupils and it is established as a higher medium, the devotion of one's life to which is now called philosophy.

There is no contradiction between the deep irony and the cheerfulness in Plato's *Dialogues*. He has stylized the trial of Socrates as a classical tragedy, because the accused has no option but to make his rational defence, and this cannot but bring him condemnation and death. He rushes to his destruction like a tragic hero, but with his eyes open, in full awareness of what he is doing. His fate is not that blind destiny which tragedy laments, but reason. So it even shines out with the radiance of reason, loses its tragic sting and takes on *meaning*. Interpreted as martyrdom it becomes 'good news'.

No doubt martyrdom also serves to give meaning, yet where in this role it radiates an aura of unquestionable authority, it shows how dubious it is. *Martyrein* means to bear witness and to swear to. But to swear to something is not just, say, to swear before a court that in the case of X this or that took place; what is also sworn to is the credibility of the authority by which one swears. The oath may well serve as a sober confirmation of facts, but it is also a magical act. And the extreme case of the witness, the martyr, is not wholly free from this ambiguity. By swearing to his idea he also makes it as true and as holy as he holds it to be. This can be an expression of sheer despair, but it can also be something which one should not really be talking about in connection with so serious a matter, calculation.

Nietzsche, with his over-sensitive nose for anything tabu and bizarre, smelt it and expressed it in his headstrong way: 'The martyrdom of the philosopher,' he claims, 'compels into the light the agitator and actor that lies concealed in him,'[6] and for him the master martyr was Socrates. Is anyone who goes to his death as deliberately and with such self-assurance as Socrates, holding all the threads of argument and action in his hands, who takes the rational example that he is making so far that he even refuses to leave prison, and *compels* the Athenians to execute him, foreseeing what deep shame and repentance his death will bring about, *suffering* his martyrdom? No, says Nietzsche, he is staging it, and thus it loses something of its seriousness. Where one supposes there to be the most truthful and purest thing that a human history overflowing with lies and dirt has to offer, ulterior motives are in play; effects are being calculated, so thoroughly that this person does not shrink even from the sacrifice of his own life to achieve the desired effect. One's own death as a means of suggesting the truth of one's own teaching and silencing all doubt about it through reverence; the truth thus enthroned again as a means of making one's own person immortal: that is the metaphysical horse-trading that Nietzsche sees Socrates pulling off almost to perfection – the secret of the success of any idolizing of ideas.

Nietzsche's sweeping antipathy to martyrs is connected with the fact that he did not want to see his own philosophizing ('that long slow pain which takes time, in which we are so to speak burned with green wood'[7]) as martyrdom at any price. But even his crudest injustices to Socrates still have an element of clear-sightedness; it cannot wholly be denied that there is a certain trend towards auto-stylization and autosuggestion in Socrates' person. Nor are they simply cunning sophistry. Rather, Socrates found himself in an inimitable state of suspension in which setting the stage for oneself is no fiction, but brings out what actually *is*: an unprecedented self-assurance and relaxation which shows its whole strength in the face of death, and which the fragile Nietzsche deeply envied.

By contrast, to the degree that it declared its martyrs blessed, Christianity also inspired a bliss of martyrdom for which subsequently it did not want to be responsible. 'Let me be food for the wild beasts,' writes Ignatius of Antioch in his Letter to the Romans, 'through them I may come to God. I pray that they will be found prompt with me; I shall even entice them to devour me immediately,' and 'Should they not consent voluntarily, I shall force them.'[8] For the church, this was soon too much of a good thing: to bring martyrdom on oneself was said to tempt God. This was consistent only if what the New Testament promised was really true: 'Whoever loses his life for my sake will gain it' (Matt. 16.25). Anyone who, speculating on this gain, actively provoked martyrdom instead of humbly waiting to see whether or not it would come about, was really only being honest about the trade-off which is secretly always an element in the thought of the Christian martyrs: one is exchanging earthly life for heavenly life.

The notion of an infinitely rewarding exchange is inherent in the Christian interpretation of martyrdom. Anyone who gives what is most precious by earthly criteria gets something even more precious in return. Unbefitting though it may be for us today to disparage the courage and steadfastness of the martyrs, we must not forget the 'incentive' which helped to strengthen their characters – and which could therefore so easily turn into sheer calculation, because it already had an element of calculation in it. To the masochistic variant that one can be quite sure of purchasing bliss through martyrdom, there later came to be added the sadistic church-political one. Whole armies of crusaders were recruited with an appeal to the precious heavenly reward of martyrdom, and this was used in the Thirty Years' War to recruit troops against the enemy confession; down to the present day it continues to be used to stir up war parties. It is only a tiny step from the personal respect which a martyr commands to the universal praise of martyrdom. However, when spelt out, that means an agreement over the victims which are now the price of the establishment of a message of salvation. They are accepted all the more easily, the more certain it seems that this message will win in the end.

Martyrdom can only be a triumph on credit for such a final victory. So it is very questionable whether the one whose last cry on the cross the evangelist reports as 'My God, why have you forsaken me?' (Matt. 27.46) was a martyr like those who later died in his name. Jesus, too, perished for his cause, but possibly in such a way that he also experienced its downfall as his own, his faith as unconfirmed, as a failure – as erroneous faith. For what he had wanted to embody and force through by his symbolic actions and parables was the kingdom of God as the saving end of history; what came was the church, which proclaimed his failure as a victory and disseminated belief in his triumphal return, bringing salvation at the end of history. The *imitatio*

Christi in which Christian martyrs believed that they were engaged perhaps has no more to do with the historical Jesus than the historical church has to do with the expected kingdom of God.

Only where someone suffers death for his convictions without the least certainty that his convictions will survive him and exalt him does any incentive, any calculation, any posing cease; only then is martyrdom taken completely seriously – so seriously that it cannot even be praised. Before someone who ventures his life for his convictions, even at the risk that as a result of his death they will become meaningless, go unheard or fail, in other words at the risk that his venture was completely in vain, one can only fall silent as before something that is holy. No comparison, no weighing of pros and cons, no justification of the content of the convictions is in place here. Not even the recommendation to imitate. If Jean Meslier, priest of a small village in the archdiocese of Rheims at the time of Louis XIV, did his pastoral duties correctly all his life and entrusted his real thoughts only to his testament, which ran to more than a thousand pages, namely that 'what is put on offer and practised in the world as worship and devotion is nothing but error, deception, imagination and deceit',[9] *he* is not the one to be accused of secretiveness and a double life, but rather the Christian society which forced him to it. That he was not inclined to go to the stake for his conviction that there is nothing but matter, neither a God nor a life after death, and preferred to end the only life in which he believed as pleasantly and as peacefully as possible, acquainting only posterity with his thoughts, is to be respected as much as the external or internal emigration of those who did not want to fall victim to Fascism or Stalinism – if the 'inner' world really was an inner world, and not another word for assimilation.

While it is unjust to require martyrdom of anyone, the insight is correct that if no one is any longer prepared to risk disadvantage, suffering or, in extreme cases their life, for their convictions, then opportunism has triumphed. Whether martyrdom is any use remains to be seen; that it is damaging where it becomes a cult is certain; but where it simply ceases without the world becoming so good that it is unnecessary, a state has been reached in which no one could trust anyone else any longer about the way. However, to the degree that the instability and disintegrating power of the modern social process have robbed of their certainty all higher ideas in which their supporters took refuge for centuries, the incentive to sacrifice oneself for them has also been lost. The certainty of being supported by a religious or political movement which will survive their own existence and which far outstrips their own ideas can lead individuals to grow beyond themselves in courage and bravery and stimulate others to do so. But such movements are no longer held together by martyrdom, and it is good that this should be so; where they owe themselves to martyrdom alone, nowadays they are usually breeding-grounds of dark superstition. The times when one could hope to move the world by martyrdom are over. Modernity is also fast-moving in that it no longer leaves any time for the formation of a tradition and a culture around someone who bore witness to his cause with his body and his life.

That makes all the more important those many people, too little known, easily forgettable and anonymous, who have also borne 'witness' in this century, sometimes not even for a particular idea, but simply against outrageous events and conditions. Real outrage does not calculate, and anyone whom it enables to struggle against the encompassing rule of force has done not only what is most necessary, but more than could ever be expected of him. For example the by no means few people who, after 1945, soon moved from Fascist prisons into Stalinist prisons, survived as the persecuted opposition in the socialism of the Eastern block and today are ignored because their resistance was not what the victors of 1989 thought, are among the most hopeful that our age which is so poor in perspectives has to offer.

Prayer

Recently, when an Australian bush fire, driven by unfavourable winds and beyond the capacity of any fire-fighting equipment, moved towards Sydney, one of the firemen conceded, 'Now we can only pray.' The man did not say what else he thought about prayer, but in his situation even a confessed atheist would have been able to say, 'My God, not that!' Where all technological means fail and one helplessly watches the catastrophe approaching, suddenly one of those archaic situations develops in which, thousands of years ago, prayer may initially have arisen. Terror and helplessness are its parents, the heartfelt sigh is its embryonic form, and where it succeed in articulating itself clearly, it acts as a magic spell which pleads for a hearing. Prayer presupposes that there are forces in nature which can be addressed, which understand human language, and which can accede to the wishes expressed in it. Prayer attempts to relate to these forces – and to that degree was once itself part of the first, undirected efforts by human beings to control nature.

While people did not yet know how to protect themselves against storms, heat and cold, how to get water and avoid drought, how to escape from lions and catch bears, how to distinguish poisonous fruits from edible fruits and cultivate the latter, prayer was as natural a factor in gaining a livelihood as hunting and collecting, sowing and reaping – and it was not clear whether the practical measures taken towards self-preservation were successful because of the prayer which accompanied them or the prayer because of them. At all events, the initial phase of prayer is a state of indecision, in which thought and action, imagination and reality, subject and object have not yet clearly been separated, and therefore what Freud called the 'omnipotence of ideas' rules, although the real issue is the impotence of these ideas. The problem is an inability to assess oneself, ignorance of one's own scope and possible influence, which at this stage makes wishes so boundless that they seem capable of commanding anything.

Thinking, wishing and praying were initially one, and the division of the world into a profane and a secular sphere was unknown. The two part company to the degree that thought learns to assess and to manipulate a external nature which is different from itself and thus becomes more than mere wishing: an arsenal of firm convictions and identifications which *are* controllable at any time and *bring* things under control. The sure control of things corresponds to one's wishes precisely because it is more than a mere wish: it is something that has proved itself by coming up against resistance, against other objects. Where such a trial takes place, where thanks to human skill an area of nature which can be controlled begins to stand out from nature which cannot be controlled, the contours start to form what is later distinguished from the sacred sphere as the profane sphere. From now on the profane sphere grows proportionately to the forces of material and intellectual productivity. Accordingly prayer loses its omnipresence. Where it allies itself with sacrificial and symbolic actions, solemn rites and dances, it already has its own precinct. It is limited to the sacral sphere: it is no longer thoughts and wishes generally, but merely a form of them.

However, it is a form which stands out. Prayer as ceremony, as ritual, was a matter for shamans, priests, rulers, kings – a high privilege. To know the formulae of prayers was to know how to rule: not just an imaginary power to conjure up deities and to influence the collective, but also real power to curse, to judge, to exterminate people. And in all this the knowledge of how to pray was not just humbug disseminated by the will to power, but also a prototype of knowledge. Getting to know the forces of procreation and growth, the stellar constellations or the regularities in the succession of seasons was inseparable from the attentiveness which the reverence of prayer showed to them, and in so doing identified regularities which gave a basis and an orientation to human existence.

Knowledge is power. This intimation was already had by prayer long before it became a formula for Bacon and a slogan for the workers' movement. However, the fate of knowledge through prayer was that to the degree that it proved itself to be verifiable experiential knowledge it became profane – in other words, it emancipated itself from prayer. And what remained of prayer itself? The experience that all the knowledge that proceeded from it was not enough to fulfil the primal wish that it had already uttered as a sigh: to do away with the alien otherness and terror of nature. Thus prayer seems like a relic of primal times in the present: it does not cease to recall how human beings feel lost in nature and appeal to its human-like features.

In the course of its long history this appeal has developed its own imagery: the idea of higher beings who are nevertheless like human beings, who protect and rescue human existence if it behaves in accordance with their will. Prayer is the attempt to penetrate this will, to fathom it and to influence it, to adapt oneself to it and it to oneself. There is no prayer which does not seek to be heard. Even the innocent 'Give us this day our daily bread' seeks to bend God to one's will and secretly presupposes that he can be bribed.

Except that initially, venality was nothing shameful, but something which still struck Benjamin about Kafka's court officials: 'The fact that they can be bribed is the only hope that humanity can cherish when faced with them.'[10] Indeed, it is the fact of allowing themselves to be addressed and moved by human imploring that made the gods like human beings at all, and thus constituted their divinity. Only to the degree that they were vacillating and corruptible were they accessible at all, did they exist. Only when the vague ideas that human beings had of them crystallized into firm characters which were seen to appear in certain laws and regularities; when the gods took on the role of an unconditionally just jurisdiction; when reliability, incorruptibility and constancy became the insignia of their credibility and vacillation a threat to them, did God's readiness to yield become the moral disrepute at which Kant turned up his nose:

> Prayer, thought of as an inner formal service of God and hence as a means of grace, is a superstitious illusion (a fetish-making); for it is no more than a stated wish directed to a Being who needs no such information regarding the inner disposition of the wisher; therefore nothing is accomplished by it ... hence God is not really served.[11]

Early Christianity had already laboured over that. If God was everything that people believed that they knew him to be, namely eternal, omnipotent, just, gracious and concerned for the salvation of each individual, wasn't it completely superfluous not only to put private wishes to him, but also to make the impudent attempt to meddle in his rule of the world? It seems absurd that the church father Augustine addresses his famous *Confessions*, which depict his wasted life on the paths of vice and error up to the point of his saving conversion, to the omnipotent God, to the only one to whom he need not have made it. Yet Augustine did this deliberately. He did not see how he could avoid the aforementioned impudence unless he transformed prayer from an request into a stock-taking, and the traditional deity to whom special wishes were addressed into a mirror of self-reflection which showed him the true meaning of the experiences of his youth.

Thus the first literary autobiography came into being. It takes the form of a prayer, but in it prayer is far from being a simple, unguarded petition. It makes great, artistic circuits of reflection and leads one to believe that the human being cannot reasonably want anything other than what God grants him; that the true prayer is that of thanksgiving – making us forget that any thanks honestly meant is thanks for the fulfilment of a wish, even where more is granted than was ever wished for. The prayer which has become reflective narrative and has been purified so that it is thanksgiving nevertheless remains, in all its subtlety, an echo of that vital imploring and wishing that it may not perceive itself to be. In order to be able to face itself, it denies its origin.

The basic principle of prayer seems to lie in the Our Father: 'Thy will be done'. This laconic petition could be interpreted simply as pure surrender to destiny – were it not that it would only make sense to pray for something which has been envisaged beforehand, and that this petition is preceded by another one, 'Thy kingdom come.' However, this can also mean 'Thy kingdom come (in order that finally) thy will may be done.' In other words, as long as this kingdom, salvation from all suffering, is not present, it has not come about at all. This bold reading has equally bold models: Abraham, who appeals to God not to destroy Sodom, 'Far be it from thee to do such a thing, to slay the righteous with the wicked' (Gen. 18.25); Moses, who beseeches him, 'Turn from thy fierce wrath and repent of this evil against thy people ... to whom thou didst swear by thine own self and didst say to them, "I will multiply your descendants as the stars of heaven"' (Ex. 32.12f.). Here too there is praying and beseeching, but with an unprecedented nuance: not to persuade God to fulfil a special wish, but to bring him to himself. As long as

God is as beside himself as he appears to be, he is not God – he *is* not.

This image already verges on atheism in the Old Testament, but this is an atheism which as it were restores their natural right to the imploring and wishing which from of old have been elements of prayer. As long as 'the creation sighs' (Rom. 8.22), prayer does not cease. No one has formulated its basic text more precisely than Nietzsche: 'Woe says, Begone! But joy would have eternity.'[12] Longingly as this text has sought its fulfilment, all the higher powers which it summoned for this purpose have distorted it. As soon as it is addressed to such a power, prayer stands under a curse: either it discredits this power as corruptible, vacillating or having failed itself in some other way, or it discredits itself as an attempt at bribery. But if whether there are divine ears to hear the basic text of the prayer is more questionable than ever, it is all the more important that human ears should become more keenly attuned to this text and not cease to pick it out from all the cunning, hardened, compulsive, auto-suggestive and mass psychotic forms that prayer has assumed under its curse in the course of history. Prayer itself needs its curse to be shaken off, and its basic text, scribbled over a thousand-fold, to be worked out. And if this could be done perfectly only by a God, the categorical imperative to make reality match it as far as is possible is still good common sense.

Charisma

There is hardly a modern head of government whom the Opposition does not accuse in the first clash in parliament of being a weak leader. That is remarkable. Democracy should be that form of state in which the people rule and the government carries out its will, but it is felt that the chief executive should be a genuine 'leader' – as if we have not had enough hair-raising experiences with this species. The complaint about weak leadership is a call for a strong man, and the never-ending longing for such a man is the other side of a will of the people which is far removed from articulating itself in such a clear, concentrated and competent way that it really makes the government its representatives and executive organs – which is what they claim to be in election campaigns.

The weaker and less clear the will of the people, the more plausible is the notion of the helmsman who knows the right course and has the competence and power to steer it. It is fearful to think that the ship is wallowing directionless, and that the crew is doing no more than surmounting the next wave. Therefore anyone who wants power must look a little like such a helmsman. Moreover, marking the voting paper is far less an act of delegation than one of trust. On the one hand it is an act of submission, which is why it is so important for the candidate in an election to give the appropriate paternal, maternal or impetuously heroic image. On the other hand it is an act of protest against the labyrinth of pressures and bureaucracy in which politics is increasingly losing itself. The head of government as an executive officer is only one more wheel in this machinery, whereas as leader he would be the human power which directs it; replaces administrative and technical procedures with a personal touch; shows those under him a goal instead of merely administering them; and arouses the forces to achieve that goal.

In addition he must have that certain something noted by Max Weber, which was already the speciality of 'the magician and the prophet', as of the 'chosen commander in war, bandit leader, condottiere', and which also survives down to modernity and the present 'in the form first of the free "demagogue" and then of the parliamentary "party leader"', namely charisma. The charismatic is 'the leader of men who is inwardly "called"', at whose disposal people put themselves, 'not by virtue of custom and constitution, but because they believe in him'.[13] To the degree that modern democracy results in an administered world, it keeps alive the wish for charismatic leaders who will breathe living spirit into their dead apparatus or simply sweep it away and replace it with a new covenant of human proximity and immediacy.

Here it is as easy to forget that the charisma of modern leaders can only communicate itself and impose itself by means of gigantic media circuses, and thus itself depends on a touch of the apparatus of the cultural industry which is so reviled, capable of being switched on and off like a sports film or an advertising spot, as it is to forget the origin of the concept of charisma in the New Testament, where initially it was by no means clearly attached to political and religious leadership. Granted, the apostle Paul imagined the divine grace *(charis)* as a power beyond the senses, but it was one that was to realize itself physically in the senses, in *gifts* of grace (charisms). These include ecstatic stammering, which evidently went the rounds among the first Christians and even entered the story of Pentecost as 'speaking in foreign tongues', and the gift of translating such stammering into comprehensible language, the gift of prophetic speech, the power of faith, healing the sick and, as a quite special gift of grace, love, without which all 'tongues of men and of angels' would be 'sounding brass and a tinkling cymbal' (I Cor. 13). The catalogue is not complete, and seems partial, as if it were sketching the church hierarchy which was later read out of it, when it lists one after the other apostles, prophets, teachers, miracle workers, those who heal the sick and those who speak in tongues (I Cor. 12.28). However, it then also strikes up yet other tones: as a member of his or her community, each Christian is something special, namely 'a member' of the 'body of Christ', an indispensable organ in a social organism the Christian character of which consists in overturning the values which prevail in the world: 'those parts of the body which we think less honourable we invest with the greater honour', because 'God gives the greater honour to the inferior part' (I Cor. 12.23f.).

Charisma

The organism as the image of a human community is part of the fixed repertoire of demagogy. The cunning statesman Menenius Agrippa in ancient Rome explained to the rebellious plebeians that just as the stomach has to be fed by the work of the other organs if the human body is to be capable of life, so in the social body the patricians have to be fed by the work of the plebeians. Livy tells us that they agreed with this brilliant inspiration. Menenius Agrippa wove the simple basic pattern of an ideology which has continued to have an effect to the present day, because it has a fatal fact on its side. Human beings are social beings; therefore their mutual dependence does not cease even in a state ruled by force. The masters live on the work of the slaves, just as the slaves live on the crumbs which fall from the masters' tables. No social order is so rotten that in times of ferment demagogues cannot wheel in the fact that all are dependent on one another, that all are in the same boat, to emphasize that the people are a community or that all of them have responsibility. And that is true: no society functions without co-operation, even if this has to be enforced. Except that enforced co-operation is a caricature of itself; only the free interaction of self-determined activities would be collaboration in the full sense of the word. Co-operation calls for social harmony. To act as though this were already established, while all tacitly continue the existing enforced co-operation, is the demagogic trick to which the ideology of the social organism gives a very long life.

However, no ideology is without a grain of truth. Can one depict the harmony of many different parts within a whole better than through the image of a healthy organism? As long as relationships are not foisted on this image which mock it, there is nothing defamatory about it. In Paul, though, it changes colour like a chameleon: sometimes it is subordinated to the existing reality, and at others held up against it as an ideal to be achieved only in the supernatural realm, only by God. Taken as a fact, the 'body of Christ' is the primitive church which really exists, a human, all too human, association of small communities with all the frictions which arise wherever a loose collection of people is tightening itself up to become an institution; and in the charisms listed above, of the apostolate, prophetic speech, teaching, etc., there are the first signs of a hierarchy of offices which are to give structure and durability to the association as soon as possible. But in so far as this 'body' stands for the overturning of the existing values of the world, in the course of which 'what is weak in the world' is 'to shame the strong' (I Cor. 1.27), mission or turning the world into the church means transforming it into a social organism which unconditionally deserves this name: in a word, the world revolution. The personal individual gift that each brings with him from the start becomes a charisma as soon as it enters into this process. No one is so insignificant, unskilled, damaged, that he has nothing to contribute to it.

To modern ears that sounds like a propaganda text-book for the establishment of socialism: swear in the masses to pursue a tremendous goal, and on the pretext that it is important for every single one, ruthlessly exploit all their strength and enthusiasm. Except that such propaganda speaks more truth than one might like:

in the struggle against conditions in which everything does not depend on the individual, it does in fact depend on each individual. And it is also the case that in the conditions of epoch-making revolutions, the construction of a new world, gifts and forces can be released which had no place in the system of co-ordinates of the old, which were u-topian in the literal sense because they did not arouse any inspiration: capacities which cannot be credited to profession, career or reputation, yet would nevertheless be the indispensable ferment of any human proceedings.

Gifts are not just a physical and social dowry, but also relate to the goal in view. Everyday life in a secondary school is by no means the worst example of how mass gifts go to waste under the conditions of a loss of a collective perspective. The 'great refusal', once a slogan of critical intellectuals, is practised there in a reflex and (self-)destructive way by millions of children and young people who do not care about politics and intellectualism. Had these kids, pumped full of narcotics of every kind but inwardly empty, a real goal, it would doubtless have the effect on them of unleashing inspiring, unpredictable capacities. That means that we must be all the more sceptical about all those who regard the lack of such a goal as a gap in the market. As long as they promote higher goals as if they were detergents, they are all rabble-rousers and are continuing to supply narcotics on the pretext of waking people up.

Already in Paul the charisma fluctuates between being a narcotic and stirring things up. The unleashing of quite inexhaustible energies which drove him to the almost superhuman achievement of his missionary journeys in the eastern Mediterranean are due to his *idée fixe* that the end-time had dawned and would reach its supernatural conclusion with the imminent return of Christ. In such circumstances, that all charisms are to serve to 'build up the community' (I Cor. 14) can always have two meanings: both the institutionalization of the church and the shaking up of existing circumstances, the pastoral edification of the cultic community and revolutionary action. And depending on their shade, preachers tend to read either the one or the other out of their key witness. He offers both.

Charisma can mean an office given from above, like that of the apostle, who feels that he has been personally appointed by God, claims the authority to command his community and evades any control because the divine Spirit cannot be determined. But charisma can also mean the energy which is released by the perspective of a better world, and anyone can develop this 'charisma from below'. There is no need of any higher legitimation for it, only the certainty that the existing wretched situation of humanity mocks its material and cultural achievements, its technological and cultural possibilities. Only if there is a sense and a feeling about this disproportion which turns into spiritual tension is charisma the driving force of humanity and its inspiration, and not humbug. If charismatics today still attribute their gifts to divine powers, they are as suspect of demagogy as if they talk a perspectiveless society into a perspective and want to trim it to aims which it does not have. However, here it is, of course, quite correct that aimlessness and decay in small things, as in great, go most closely together. There are no counter-forces against this tendency without charismatic sparks. Where all charisma disappears, a lack of perspective is inevitable and all days become evenings.

Tabu

There are no longer any real tabus. What we call tabus today are no longer what the Polynesian word 'tabu' once meant: something that is 'marked out', special, something that is inherent in particular persons, things, actions, states, say a state of trance or the food of the shaman; the menstruating woman; the place, elements and course of the offering of a sacrifice; the custom of mating with one's own children, parents, brothers and sisters. Tabus are the uncovered nerve centres of a collective which one cannot attack without upsetting the whole order to which it is felt to belong. Those who do that themselves become 'tabu'; they must be segregated (as a rule expelled or killed) to restore order.

A genuine tabu is something that is taken for granted. It has never been agreed, justified, taught or even written down, and yet a long process of common experience has instilled it in the flesh and blood of a collective to such a degree that it strikes out like a conditioned reflex against those who attack it. The 'don't touch me' of the tabu is the first categorical imperative of humankind.

It is as though the primitives governed by tabus already knew Nietzsche's 'What first has to be proved is of little value'.[14] For where one begins to seek reasons for a tabu, it is no longer a matter of course; it is no longer regarded as categorical, since thought has already ushered in that process of erosion which finally no longer leaves any prohibition, any custom, any norm alone and takes it for granted. Moreover gods began their careers in human thought as reasons for tabus ('You shall not kill, shall not commit adultery, etc.', *because* God wills it) and in time themselves needed to be justified ('How can God will what he allows to happen?). Finally even their existence had to be demonstrated ('How can there be a God in the face of all the terrible things that are happening?'). Here, too, 'What first has to be proved is of little value.' Proofs of God already belong to the twilight of the gods. The perspicacity that they strive for is a expression of the doubt that they are meant to dispel. But even the most prominent modern descendant of the gods, Kant's categorical imperative, did not fare better. Far removed from being a matter of course (a whole *Groundwork of the Metaphysics of Morals* had to be written to justify it), it rather aroused doubt in the possibility of categorical principles, i.e. those which are intrinsically so utterly valid that no quest for new, 'better' moral principles has since then been able to stifle them.

In short, there are no longer authentic, original tabus; there is none that has not already been battered by discussion and is not already undermined by arguments, that does not have holes which are stopped up with pretexts. However, the 'don't touch me' of the old tabus does live on in this stuffed form, more or less skilfully prepared and fed with arguments. It no longer strikes out as blindly as it does with primitive people who fall upon deviants without reflection, for the modern spirit of the Enlightenment has practised it knowingly – but in this way that spirit has also been able to maintain it *against* its better knowledge. The old collective which stoned the man who made his mother pregnant was cruel; the modern Islamic state power which has two lovers flogged if it catches them being intimate is cynical. It *knows* that its tabu is untenable, and it is its furious struggle against this knowledge which makes the tabu driven by reflection strike out no less vigorously than the old authentic one once did.

Because modern tabus have been equipped and padded with ideas to the point that they deny themselves, the location of the nerve centres which are still most similar to what was originally called tabu is now really uncertain. First of all, tabus used to be associated with sexuality. And there was good reason for this: in any tabu there is a suppression of drives which, if left unbridled, threaten what a collective feels to be its order and its support. Unregulated pleasure is one of the unconditional enjoyments which neither takes heed nor calculates; it devotes, surrenders itself to a cause, a person or an event, and forgets itself in being fascinated and fulfilled. It can be as completely harmless as the consuming of a piece of fruit; if it takes hold of a person or a cause which is not entitled to it, it can be loaded with tension or destructive in the exercise of its own vengeance. Pleasure is asocial and amoral in three senses: it does not bother about the social structure; it threatens it; and it points beyond it. For all pleasure 'wants eternity', as Nietzsche remarked or, as Augustine said, is 'fragrance that breathing does not disperse', 'tasting what eating does not diminish' and 'clinging where satiety does not divorce'.[15]

Eternal bliss would be an amoral state – like its extreme opposite, total anarchy. Common to both would be freedom from the straitjacket of all norms. The sexual excesses which were celebrated in ancient temples after the sacred marriage of heaven had something of this atmosphere. Pleasure has an impulse which is as anarchical as it is mystical. No society can allow it without regulation, but none can it satisfy it either. The relationship of society to individual desire always remains a violent one, even if it prunes the drives like a gardener, not only mutilating but also cultivating them. So the key question to any society is: How much pleasure does it make possible? How much pleasure does it tolerate?

An intolerable amount, anxious morality watchers today tell us; one need only look at the obscenities and violence which flicker over television screens every day. Exhibitionists and child pornographers are spreading into chat shows; no sexual part is left undiscussed; no practice of sex and murder is faded out in the feature films with which cinemas and commercial television stations feverishly attract customers. The last tabus are tottering, society is sinking into anarchy. Save civilization, and ban this trash!

Now it is still questionable to what degree the brutality on television screens nowadays really prompts imitation and how far it is simply a way of finding a release for blocked drives, just as earlier it proved over-hasty merely to see pornography as a stimulus towards rape. But even if in a medium which hour after hour, day after day, broadcasts sex and crime, and even to children, the danger of stimulation needs to be taken far more seriously than pornographic photography, one thing is certain: there can be no question here of this being a socially relevant breach of tabu. This is not yet the end of culture, but a consequence of the entertainment industry which, as competition sharpens, has to fight ever more keenly for customers. It is quite simply a matter of the ratings, and here sex and crime are the best bet. Some people get their ongoing thrills from indignation at the sexual or aggressive intoxication of others without getting involved in any way, all the more so, the less it has anything to do with their own experience of pleasure. And those who greedily watch the falling of the last veils before the camera hardly notice any more something of which they are really well aware; that the decisive tabu on the media has not been loosened in the slightest by this. The pleasure which is offered is a pre-packaged, filtered, tailored one: it is that of the voyeur who seeks to compensate himself for something that escapes him by gaping.

The voyeur is the prototype of modern pleasure. Even where this pleasure is experienced actively, and not just looked at from the outside, there is a tendency to take part in it *like* a voyeur, to use it *like* a TV set. How does that happen? In a society which only survives because the majority of its members sell their physical and mental capacities for a few hours a day in the interest of others, thus doing what was once regarded as the essence of prostitution, there is a connection between pleasure and the economy about which Freud's talk of 'earning pleasure' is more illuminating than he himself was aware. It opens up an attitude to life which finds business profitably done so pleasant that conversely it also begins to see the enjoyment of pleasure in terms of profit. However, anyone who pursues pleasure like profit, as something that one can put down on the credit side, is haunted by the feeling of having too little, of having been done down. More than ever before, this feeling is associated with the present experience of pleasure. No society has made more pleasure possible than modern society. It has prepared a whole set of machinery to relieve people of activities which they do not enjoy. But to the degree that people function as appendages to this machinery rather than controlling it, their pleasure, too, takes on a mechanical, instrumental, machine-like aspect. And mechanized pleasure is sterilized; however much it may have its fling – and a society no longer obligated to any fixed family structures *allows* this – it is deprived of its anarchical mystic roots and thus of its best. The excess may still take place, larded with everything for which the word 'perverse' stands, but from now on it has sobered down. It is now a matter of violently letting off steam, regulating the household of desires. It has no power, either good or bad, to explode society.

No matter how repugnant the new wave of obscenities on the television and how infuriating the Benetton advertisement with the picture of a shot Serbian soldier may be, at the level of society as a whole the conventions which are broken here have only the status of private whims and sensibilities; they are not nerve centres which have to be kept intact if society is to continue. We find those more in that unsexual traffic which takes place on the roads and in the labour market. Television cameras may focus undeterred on the victims of wars, earthquake and hunger, but the bodies of those killed in road accidents, especially in one's own country, are only shown covered up. No one is to be put in the position of having to identify individuals, even their next of kin. We all know the approximate number of those who die on the roads each year – but the transport of goods and people is so essential for society that a serious intervention here, a refusal to accept the toll of blood which it levies each year, would mean the collapse of society. And for all the stress that it has meanwhile come to bring with it, taking part in this elixir of life has still not ceased to be experienced as pleasure. There is nothing with which the feeling of autonomy is so intrinsically bound up as it is with the car. The lack of mobility is felt as impotence in just the same way as the lack of a job. In a society which has allegedly become shameless, countless people are ashamed of their economic inferiority, just as people used to be ashamed only of a physical defect or a crime. And where there is such vigorous, mass shame, there may most likely still be something that deserves the name tabu.

That persons, things, ideas, feelings are tenable only so far as they 'count' forms the nerve centre or nerve centres in a society which is engaged in producing commodities. Of course, everyone says that this is not the case; that human beings are more than things; that the unemployed, the old and the sick are just as much people as those capable of functioning. But how deeply

44

is that still believed? It is not just that those concerned experience things differently; we need only see what happens once anyone really touches this nerve centre seriously, as once when a handful of foolhardy people, the Red Army Faction, declared war on capitalist society because of its inhumanity. In almost a knee-jerk reaction, in a flash people united as a collective to attack the deviants, and the disproportion between actual threat and public hysteria showed that what was being touched on here was really tabu. Society might be well padded against protest and critical theory, but it was sensitive enough to react like a fury to the first actual contact.

Against this background it becomes clear in a flash how little breaking of tabus there is in the new right-wing radicalism. Hardly had it been able to credit itself with a spontaneous wave of sympathy in the population than a certain terror at so much guilelessness and good will set in, caused by second thoughts. However, National Socialism is a nerve centre of the first order in the German self-understanding. This sort of thing must never happen again, say the great majority, and many people today who are between forty and sixty years of age mean that so seriously that hardly anything affects them more deeply than when their own children and pupils raise their hands in the Hitler salute. Thus superficially these young people are breaking a complacent tabu when they shock those around them with Nazi symbols that have been compromised all over the world, with gangs and attacks on foreigners. But the background to this is an anxiety of being swamped by foreigners, the need to put a stop to immigration and the new national self-consciousness, which is far too close to the feeling of broad masses of people for anything like popular anger to break out against it.

To the degree that healthy popular feeling, which calls for lynchings when something goes against it, soberly and sorrowfully classifies the young right-wing radicals as 'misguided' and claims that they are using worthless means for debatable ends, that they are grubby pioneers of a clean policy of German self-assertion, their breach of tabu is excused as rashness. They have dashed ahead impetuously and in excessively headstrong obedience on the way indicated by economic development, which is opening up an ever wider gap between the oases of high technology and the deserts of structural weaknesses, unemployment and mass emigration. They think the state of the German economy better than it is. However, regardless of this, nationalism and xenophobia are not in the least what attacks the central nervous system of a society to which sale and competition have become second nature.

Where superficial tabus are torn down, underlying ones are often stuffed and fed. One popular pose on the political scene is now to present oneself as a tabu-breaker, i.e. a bold, enlightened person. Edzard Reuter recently called for 'unrestricted thinking' along the lines of Hannah Arendt, and then continued: 'We will not be able to avoid a two-digit (sic) unemployment figure even if the general situation should lead to a manifest recovery', saying that 'of course ... our wages are too high', and finally that 'our bloated social administrations should be forced to go on a slimming course', that it is time for 'drastic cuts in the public sector' and second thoughts about the majority suffrage and the status of professors as civil servants.[16]

So speaks a great tabu-breaker of today, with refreshing honesty and pertinence compared with the average political speeches. However, for all his bold attacks on professional associations, lobbies and politicians, his sole concern is that the nervous system of the world economic order should not be attacked, though the first step in serious 'unrestricted thinking' should be to give an account of its tabu character. Here a precise distinction needs to be made between unnecessary and unavoidable oppression, and then between unnecessary and indispensable tabus. The tabu on rape, murder and killing will always be part of dignified dealings between human beings; the occurrence of these things can never completely be excluded as long as men and women are frustrated beings who can be disappointed, although there are all the technological and cultural possibilities for social conditions in which such actions approach zero. Only eternal bliss would be a state completely free of tabus.

On the other hand, there are tabus which are completely nonsensical at the technological and cultural stage that we have attained. The way in which it is apparently taken for granted that human beings and things are to be prepared for sale as by a chemical process, and are drawn on to the market by magnets, there to fulfil or to fail their purpose, is the great 'don't touch me' of modern society. That is its general tabu, in relation to which all the other things that are still called tabus today gain their status. For tabu is not just tabu. There are some tabus which are significant for human beings as the apron strings by which the desires learn to move, and others which kill senseless pleasure; numerous tabus do not deserve the title at all because they represent no more than the quirks of individuals or groups – and finally there is that all-embracing tabu, in the field of force of which all others stand or fall. As long as this field of force is tabu, the breaking of tabus which is hawked on the market, with which films, politicians and business magnates clamour for attention, is eyewash or what Horkheimer and Adorno said of the culture industry: 'Enlightenment as mass deception'.

Possession

It was no joke when the painter Christoph Haizmann 'in the year 1669' dipped his pen in his own blood and noted: 'I sign away my soul to Satan, to be his very own son, and in nine years to give him my body and soul.' Happily he could report that shortly before the nine years were up, in his panic he went to such understanding clergymen that with their help and that of the Holy Virgin at Mariazell he got back the document: 'he saw the demon in the corner of the chapel,' the tradition assures us, 'tore himself away from the fathers who were holding him, and seized the paper in his hand'. However the painter may have engineered the miracle of Mariazell, he will hardly have fabricated the depression after the death of his father which he experienced as irresistible pressure to sign himself over to Satan, and the 'convulsive seizures and visions, loss of consciousness and painful sensations' when the end of the period threatened. So for Freud, too, who thoroughly analysed the church document about the painter, the case was clear-cut: of course he had not been possessed by the devil but by the authority of his father, the loss of which drove him into spiritual distress to the point that a regular diabolical neurosis developed.[17]

What Price Religion?

Regardless of whether one shares Freud's diagnosis in every detail, the deciphering of possession as a psychological illness was a great piece of enlightenment. One can only understand how the tormenting power which threatens to seize a person with terrible alienation does not necessarily come from outside but may arise from within as a constituent part of one's own person, although one does not want to recognize it there at any price, if one is aware how little the conscious self is master in its own house, how much it merely forms the top floor of a whole household of drives and feelings – rather like the rider on a horse which he can firmly rein in or which can run away with him.

Wishes, drives, which society has prohibited so strongly that even individuals forbid them to themselves, can also make themselves felt as obsessive or fascinating obsessions and arise as it were behind the back of the conscious self, catch it unawares or captivate it, just like spiritual violations the pain or painfulness of which is too much for conscious memory to tolerate. There is no doubt that a large part of what was called demonic possession at the end of the Christian Middle Ages consisted of such stimuli, which surfaced in the figure of the lascivious he-goat, the witches' sabbath, vampires, or other kinds of ghostly combinations of human being and animal; as a rebellion of the lower levels of the Christian soul against what its upper levels expected of it in the name of Christ, the saints and the gospel.

Modern theologians readily concede this. All the discoveries of critical psychology are highly welcome to them when it is a matter of getting rid of the devil. The devil disturbs believers and delights unbelievers. But the church no longer wants this at a time when it is short of customers. 'When we use the terms "evil", "the power of evil", we are referring to an indeterminate entity which is only in our minds, and therefore it must be said that there is no such thing as "evil"', remarks Herbert Haag.[18] And what about the power of the good? Is that also merely an indeterminate entity which is only in our minds? No, that remains what it was, the God who really exists and has been revealed in Jesus Christ. To regard the devil as a human fiction and God as valid currency so as then to be able to offer a cure for the nightmare of the devil in the name of God; that is the contribution of advanced theology to the modern hygiene of the soul, which is working towards a completely obsessionless ego.

However, this is to forget one thing. This conscious ego which is completely preoccupied in keeping itself free from all possible obsessions owes its existence to a whole series of them. It has not dropped down from heaven, but emerged from an infinitely laborious process by which the soul works itself out. There can be no self without self-discipline. It must stop being the plaything of all the momentary drives by which it is initially tossed around by nature and tame them; it must bend them so that they become elements of it, which it can control as far as possible, and it must impose itself on them as a permanent, enduring will. Even today, individuals take years to achieve this. For humankind it was a process lasting millennia: a stretch of very hard spiritual labour. It was not done voluntarily. Anxiety at the nameless terror of an overwhelming, incomprehensible nature drove it on.

This terror is the primal form of the holy. To stand up to its shattering force, human beings had to do violence to themselves: to show up this terror as an angry higher power in order to give themselves a chance to have a soothing influence on it by sacrificing all that was important to them – human beings, animals, things, their own claims. It was the spell of the holy which focussed feeling and thought on terrifying phenomena and meaningful escape from them: on the raging storm or the predatory animal; on sacred hedges, trees, stones, hills; later on mother earth, the stars or the divine spirit. In orientating itself on such fixed points thought gave itself a first firmness, 'consistency', drew its first conclusions, presented the world to itself as being everywhere a complex of meaning, 'logified' it. Just as surely as today 'convulsive seizures and visions, loss of consciousness and painful sensations' prove highly threatening to the cohesion of the conscious ego, so they once were part of the pangs of its hard birth.

We still note something of this at the summits of the high religions. What is remarkable about the great Old Testament prophets, for example, is that they cannot defend themselves against the fearful visions of disaster which they cry out against Israel. These come upon them like the roaring of a lion (Amos), a storm wind (Ezekiel), an irresistible command (Isaiah), against which no struggling and imploring helps (Jeremiah). Their unprecedented criticism, one of the boldest pieces of self-reflection in Jewish religion, emerges as a powerful religious obsession and gains its linguistic force from that.

Long before any 'evil spirit', i.e. the forbidden, the

suppressed, the split off, articulated itself as possession, it was the vehicle of 'intellect': of thought, reason, reflection. Socrates' *daimonion*, that inner voice which, while not telling him what to do, did tell him what he could accept, was of course none other than his own reason. However, it was a reason which he experienced as a higher authority in his own person: as his genius or, in modern terms, his 'guardian angel'. And the consciousness of this higher element in him gave him the incomparable assurance, ease, persistence with which he tested the wisdom of his fellow citizens, pretended or real, defended himself against the charge of the court, scorned escape from prison, and finally took the deadly cup of hemlock. He had been able to load what seemed to him to be reason with spiritual – 'libidinous' – energy to such a degree that it seemed to him to be his governing and guiding power. Had Socrates not been possessed by reason, he would not have been the living embodiment of the way in which that reason, that capacity for abstraction which distinguishes human beings from animals, can also be a determinative force in human decisions and actions.

Thought alone does not achieve this, and the most gifted intellect can run out of steam if, as Nietzsche says, 'a fine exceptional understanding is put in a base soul'.[19] The soul must set its own thoughts on fire if it is to have the energy that they need to achieve something in the world and leave it behind. Take away from Jesus of Nazareth the *idée fixe* of the imminent kingdom of God which is about to break so radically with the previous course of the world that here is nothing after it but vengeance and punishment for the injustices of history, and one has taken away the very element that constitutes the unique shape and fascination of this person and sparked off Christianity. Take away from Bacon and Descartes the obsession that humanity will become complete by deciphering all the mysteries of nature, and one has eliminated what inspired them as pioneers of the modern control of nature. What would have become of modern democracy without the obsessive euphoria over progress and human rights of the men of the Enlightenment? What would become of the compositions of Leonardo, Rembrandt and van Gogh or Mozart, Beethoven and Schubert without the possession with which they worked? 'Art does not arise from ability but from necessity', comments Arnold Schoenberg. Either it has seized the artist, drives him and compulsively breaks out of him, or it is a fad – and not art.

'Has any one at the end of the nineteenth century any distinct notion of what poets of a stronger age understood by the word *"inspiration"*?', asked someone of whom one would least have expected it.

The idea of revelation, in the sense that something which profoundly convulses and upsets one suddenly becomes visible and audible with indescribable certainty and accuracy – describes the simple fact. One has – one does not seek; one takes – one does not ask who gives: as thought suddenly flashes up like lightning, it comes with necessity, without faltering – I have never had any choice in the matter.

Everything happens quite involuntarily, as if in a tempestuous outburst of freedom, of absoluteness of power and divinity. If one had the smallest vestige of superstition left in one, it would hardly be possible completely to set aside the idea that one is the mere incarnation, mouthpiece or medium of an almighty power.[20]

That is conceded by one of the sharpest critics of religion, Nietzsche. Like some mighty relic from prehistory his experience towers over the modern world, and he himself knows how anachronistic it is. Usually it is claimed only by people who are masking the lack of intellect in their inspirations with a reference to the exalted states of their soul. A condition such as Nietzsche describes progresses formally towards a higher power which is expressed in it. However, every such power has occasion to shun the light of reason, the piercing sharpness of which is needed more urgently than ever in the face of all the revelations, communications, visitations and inspirations which are today being traded on the 'market of possibilities'.

Most of the certainty of faith which is praised there does not stand up to critical reflection for a moment. That the sects nevertheless flourish, that so many are so prone to anything which presents itself as a higher revelation, has to do with the fact that for the cog in the machine, which is what modern men and women increasingly feel themselves to be, everything that is not a function, a means to an end, relative to something else, but stands for itself and gives support and meaning, is disappearing. Thus the soberly functional moves of the market, on which value is attached only to what has a price, to what can be calculated in terms of something else and exchanged, and the arsenal of *idées fixes*, each of which presents itself in the rowdy competition of the market as the only one which brings salvation, complement each other. So-called scholars in the humanities who push around the ideas of their tradition from Plato to Freud like clerks moving files, and gurus who are possessed by the absolute validity of the Bible, the Qur'an, the stars or whatever, relate to each other as the negative to the print. They are irreconcilable opposites, but one nevertheless bears the features of the other.

No wonder that on each side pastors appear for the other: here preachers who diagnose the homeless wandering of modern rationality as *the* spiritual disease and offer their *idée fixe* as the cure for it; there psychologists who fight possession *per se* in the name of the Enlightenment and to this end outline a typology of the fanatic which steers clear of the content that has possessed him and describes him only formally – as someone who 'overvalues' a particular idea, is over-preoccupied with it emotionally, is unable and unwilling to balance it with the reality of his environment and instead is ready to use violence to implement it.

Such typology justifies itself by numerous psychological case studies which extend from the member of the sect to the football fan, from the obsession which governs the whole of life to the hobby and whim, but it is also applied to cases where it loses its grip. In the framework of such a typology, any resistance fighter who without further ado insisted on the inhumanity of Fascism and Stalinism, and was not inclined either in exile or in prison to drop this idea and assimilate to

those around him who thought otherwise; who moreover in no way saw that the renunciation of force
against a violent state is the last conclusion of wisdom,
is seen as being just as fanatical as any guru blabbering
about cosmic powers. The excessive spiritual energy
needed to hold on to a critical insight even when it is
disapproved of, when one is threatened or persecuted by
those around, may hardly be quantitatively different
from someone's obsession with fast cars, fine wines,
old postage stamps, rare beetles, blond women or the
absoluteness of his or her religious or political doctrine.
Therefore in the typology it merely counts as a case of
an 'overvalued idea', like so many others.

The unexpressed criterion of such a classification is a
diffuse democratic mean for which truth, majority and
normality mean roughly the same thing and all the
thought which critically and uncompromisingly goes to
the root of things, i.e. *radical* thought, can appear
merely as a form of over-valuing, and therefore as
fanaticism. By the criteria of democratic normality,
anyone who will not be talked out of the notion that
modern society, which systematically produces commodities and crises with a greater or lesser degree of
democracy, is heading with increasing speed towards its
own destruction unless its capitalistic global structure is
overcome, when almost everyone else has abandoned
this notion and resolved to confuse the existing world
economic order with a natural law, is simply possessed.
The unusual energy which he has to expend in order to
hold firm to his unpopular 'idea' against an oppressive
majority is an infallible sign that he is ripe for a mental
hospital.

What Price Religion?

Today it is not deemed good for people to be either gripped or possessed by thoughts. Thoughts should be represented, as vacuum cleaners and cookers are marketed by a representative who constantly changes product and firm, without his heart, let alone his person or even his life, being in the matter. However, the democratic representative of convictions is merely the negative aspect of the fanatical perpetrator of convictions. As surely as it is part of a peaceful existence to have peace with one's own soul and no longer to be tormented by obsessions, whims, fancies, so certainly there is a false release from possession: one which along with the *idées fixes* also removes those rough edges that make up a person's individuality. Moreover under the conditions of the market economy, a completely obsessionless self would end up as an ever-flexible and adaptable self, which one could also call completely characterless and expressionless.

Grace

The former Federal President several times made use of his right to pardon criminals. Recently a former member of the Red Army Faction condemned to life imprisonment was released in such a way. And again at the time the old question came up: are such gracious acts, for which the distinguished gentlemen is accountable to no one, really legitimate? A first answer is: yes, of course, the Basic Law in fact provides for them. The second answer is: no, of course not, the very essence of such a gracious act is that it is an exception to the valid law. Had it to give account of itself before a legal body, it would no longer be a gracious act.

There is no getting away from the fact that with pardon is associated a sovereign who can decide as he likes – that is why in 1791 the French Revolution struck the right of pardon from the constitution; it had had enough of that kind of sovereign. Ten years later the right was reintroduced; in the meantime people had come to know mills of justice which ground inexorably. But to claim pardon is to touch on the dark underworld from which modern civil law has grown, even in its brightest and clearest forms.

Let us have no illusions: rights were formerly privileges – that of the tribal leader to the lion's share of the booty, of the priest to the remains of the sacrifice, of the warrior caste to exemption from physical labour. Legal conditions were morals and customs established by force: regulated conditions of power. Here law played the role of a key distributor. Plato defines justice as assigning to each his due. Its even more primeval basic notion is to assign to each person what is appropriate to him, his rank or his actions; its symbol is the scales, the principle of recompensing like by like, equivalence.

But recompensing like with like also means recompensing unlike with unlike. So initially the principle of equivalence in no way brought about the demolition of privileges but prescribed them, in such a way that nature seemed to have ordained them: the more one's physical strength, the more one's rights; the more one's freedom to do as one wants. Grace derives from this free space. Only the one without rights may not do anything he wants: one can be gracious to *him*, but *he cannot* be gracious to anyone.

So for a long time law was none other than the law of grace. Because the more powerful is in the right, he can deal with the powerless, those delivered over to him, at his whim, either graciously or ungraciously. The one conditions the other. To show one's favour to someone means to withhold it from others. Rejection goes with grace, as the shadow goes with the light. The pardon which a Federal President pronounces means the rejection of countless other requests for pardon – whether they have actually been submitted in writing or whether they have never passed the stage of the involuntary sigh.

Grace

When the law of grace was the predominant legal practice, at the same time it was far more: a whole model for explaining the world. Not only were weaker men delivered over to the mercy of stronger men, but the whole human collective was at the mercy of a far more powerful nature. Consequently that was – in the right. Whatever those who guided it, the gods, imposed on human beings, they did so rightly. If it was a misfortune, then the right of the gods to recognition and veneration had obviously been disregarded; their ungracious reaction was at the same time a hint that they should be made gracious, be offered sacrifice. The sacrifice recognizes the divine anger as a right – but as a right which one can twist. If human beings succeed in assuaging wrath, they have turned ungraciousness into grace, which is now just as much a right and a well-deserved reward as its counterpart was previously.

In the law of grace, grace is not a right and yet is still a right; the right is a manifestation of favour or disfavour, and grace is a legal matter. And there is no relying on either as long as they are thought of as combined in a higher power, even if it proves as incorruptible as *moira* (= 'the distributor'), the Greek goddess of fate, for whom right, grace and disgrace are the same thing. She assigns to each his due; to this degree she is absolutely just. But she does so blindly, without awareness, and there are no reasons for what she does; to this degree her absolute justice is absolutely arbitrary. The biblical God also acts in a unity of grace and law, but this unity is full of tension: certainly as a destiny which assigns to each his due, but as a destiny which can see and which, moved by the pain of the world, directs its course for the good, a higher counsel which brings about its destiny with sheerly good purposes and reasons, except that what these are remains concealed from human reason.

This God too, however much he may have revealed himself, does not allow one to look at the cards. One may interpret the enjoyment of good fortune as his grace and misfortune as his gracious testing, which wants only the best; even eternal damnation for those who cannot appreciate this good purpose anywhere may still shine out in the light of grace as its other side. But why happiness and sorrow are divided as they are, and why the world goes on as it does, does not become any more evident. What fate sends, it sends rightly, since it is gracious; thus all earthly happiness and misery finds a higher justification which does not explain anything and has an excuse for everything. It appears as surely as Amen in church, as soon as the question is asked how the rubbish heap of history can be reconciled with the assertion of an all-wise ruler of the word; it asserts the inability of human reason to recognize the divine counsel, and nevertheless claims to know very well that this counsel is good and right.

Grace as a back door for declaring the power of facts in the last instance nevertheless to be the law: that is the basic pattern of any theological and political law of grace, and reason enough for abolishing both of them. Politically that is possible: the bourgeois democratic law that no longer wants like to be rewarded with like but wants to be the same law for all, irrespective of status, skin colour, religion, gender or income, is in fact powerfully on the advance in the modern world. Not that it is not undermined in many instances; but hardly anyone dares to speak out openly against it. For in contrast to the basis of equal basic rights for all and just recompense for their deeds, in this battle of all against all into which the modern competitive society is increasingly developing, the outbreak of open terror can hardly be prevented any more.

But how could the theological law of grace become a bourgeois democratic law? Democracy requires debate and voting on the divine plan of salvation as if it were a government proposal. Theology requires people to keep their fingers off: 'Who are you, a man, to answer back to God? Will what is moulded say to its moulder, "Why have you made me thus?" Has the potter no right over the clay, to make out of the same lump one vessel for beauty and another for menial use?' (Rom. 9.20). However much the churches today also speak of democracy – if they were really serious about it, they would have to drop the divine potter with a loud bang.

So what is still left of 'his' grace? Perhaps the best part, the human part. Grace is a humane leaven: compassion, mercy, respect, generosity, are the properties on which it draws – but these are properties which human beings can exercise only from time to time. No one can practise them constantly, and even a God could not show them round the clock without mercy becoming miserable, generosity characterless and concern sloppiness. They are only possible – and only make sense – as exceptions. And this sense arises specifically from the classical definition of justice: to each his due. This definition is formal: it does not say *what* is to be measured. To recompense each precisely according to rank, gender or confession produces only a class law, even in the most favourable instance. To recompense each exclusively according to his deeds produces bourgeois law. But what is a deed without its social context and the whole physical and spiritual constitution and disposition from which it arose? What court can shed sufficient light on this complex web or know in advance how much the perpetrators will take the punishment to heart? A sentence which one person coolly shrugs off can affect another in such a way that he is more damaged than improved by it. The deed may be proved beyond all doubt, and the customary penalty for it may be correctly given – and in a specific instance there can nevertheless be a miscarriage of justice.

In fact only a God who sees into the hearts of all could give his due to each, namely to a particular, irreplaceable individual. But because such a God cannot be perceived, and human beings are not given such perception, for its own sake justice needs grace. It cannot do by itself what it seeks to do and should do, namely to accord to each his due. It needs the exception from its rules in order to get as near as possible to the unconditionally just criterion for which it strives. Justice which despises any grace turns into self-righteousness. Grace is not a blot on justice, but its beauty spot.

With grace goes a sovereign. That remains the case even if sovereignty does not simply mean mere political power but a specifically human quality. Anyone who knows that law needs grace is inclined to treat it with the necessary mental detachment – in a sovereign way. The capacity to stand back from one's own need for retribution is no less a sign of sovereignty. In the act of grace, justice grows beyond itself: the principle of equivalence holds its breath. As surely as unpacified existence can be brought to reason only by the application of equivalents, so surely a pacified existence would be free from the pressure of lasting reciprocal calculation. Grace indicates something of this. It sets a sign – though this is an ambivalent one. Saul was relieving himself in the cave in which David was hiding from him in flight: 'Then David arose and stealthily cut off the skirt of Saul's robe' (I Sam. 24.7) instead of killing him. That was sovereign – precisely because he put at risk the power which he had been unexpectedly given over his enemy and thus his life.

Risk goes with grace. A gracious God risks nothing. Because it does not use its superiority, grace can become a fiasco if it is exploited. How many of those who spared an enemy given into their hands were later mercilessly destroyed by him! So gestures of grace can go terribly wrong. To make them a moral duty is senseless and illegitimate. Long-term grace produces corruption or burn-out. Therefore no ethic of compassion works either. Compassion as a general principle for action, and therefore at all times with all and everyone, with Hitler and all concentration camp victims and the whole animal world, becomes paralysed and is no longer distinguishable from the weakness and venality which Kant and Nietzsche suspected in it. By contrast, compassion as a momentary, spontaneous impulse is one of the finest achievements of humanity.

Where grace is practised, grace is received, but it is not practised wherever it is received. Sometimes the circumstances can prove favourable without planning, and no one can be made responsible for that. Really it is nothing but chance, in the sense of something that happens to one: not for no cause, in the scientific sense, but certainly unpredictable. To give the name grace to such chance, advantage, privilege or whatever must not mean counting it a display of personal favour from a supernatural being. First of all it simply means: I did not deserve it, there is no equivalent to account for it. At this moment grace is what the Greeks called *kairos*: the happy moment which as it were asks to be utilized and which it is irresponsible to neglect. Lessing made his *Nathan* into a whole kairology because it dawned on him that unless human reason is helped by a combination of fortunate circumstances that no reason can plan, it will never succeed in humanizing human nature and nature outside humankind.

From this perspective even reason needs grace, just as there is of course also a 'grace of late birth'. The fact that I was born only after National Socialism and did not have to face the decision to join in or emigrate, to risk my life on the front or in the resistance, is a tremendous advantage, a privilege which I have not earned in any way – just as it is a privilege to grow up in the middle-class circumstances of Central Europe instead of in a Latin America favela or to be able to make a living in more favourable circumstances than the Antarctic or the Sahara. To call such chances 'grace' is simply to want to prove worthy of them: to allow a maximum of one's own advantage to flow over to others.

Grace as the shame of justice at its own inadequacy and grace as a happy chance: each requires the other.

Grace

Just as surely as the two cannot be forced together, so it is certain that a world completely without grace is hell.

Sect

Sect is a insulting word – splinter group, scum – coined to denote those who separate themselves from the truth to which one holds firm oneself. Sectarians (= heretics) are always the others. And they are smaller groups. Sect has always been the term applied to minorities which separate themselves from a majority. One connotation is that the truth lies with the majority. The majority has the power and therefore the right to attach this insulting name to those who do not belong.

Logically, a separation is always two-sided: that of the crumbs from the loaf is also that of the loaf from the crumbs. But the perception is one-sided, depending on size, importance and power, and has led to the establishment of a linguistic rule which always has the smaller being divided from the greater, the member from the body, the individual from the collective, and never vice versa. Only when the relationship of size and power shifts does the terminology change. Christianity began as a tiny Jewish sect and Protestantism as a Christian one. Nothing but the fact that they became great and powerful secured them the recognition of being a distinctive religion or confession.

Of course minorities which split off from majorities

never regard themselves as sects. The real sectarians are not the ones who have split off from the truth, but rather the thoughtless many who have been led astray by those in power; they are not given this name simply because they are in the majority. 'Many are called, few are chosen' is the motto that the few hold up against them

Anyone who suspects that this is exclusively arrogance fails to recognize the boldness it once took to arrive at the idea that majority and truth are two different things, like power and truth. When Amos accused the Israelite leaders of putting the will of God to shame instead of embodying it; when Socrates convicted the hallowed customs and usages of Athens of being unholy; when Jesus put Jewish faithfulness to the law in the pale by calling for love of enemy; when Marx exposed the modern ideas of freedom, equality and brotherhood as masks of expression and exploitation, these individuals were setting themselves against a people, a culture, a whole society and letting them know, 'The basis of your power is speaking out against it. Your power is groundless, unjustified, untrue.'

Those who speak in this way are eloquently claiming truth for themselves – not just any truth, but the highest truth. What they regard as such may be sheer invention or have the deepest foundation – at all events it is more valuable to them than any physical power. It is something *meta*physical, as a result of which they feel themselves to be separated *from* the mass and sent *to* it. Such a person is not one of the mass – and therefore is capable of speaking for the suffering and oppressed in it. Only from the protection of a sure feeling of having been chosen did individuals and minorities begin to opt against the dominant power and for the impotent, and to the present day no individual or group is in a position to do this unless inspired by at least a touch of elitism and a sense of mission. That is why arrogance and incorruptible criticism stand so close together. Without the feeling of being rather better than the majority, no one arrives at any critical ideas. However, without these the mass does not become any better.

That explains the tense relationship of the sectarian to his own powerlessness and the powerlessness of others whom he represents. Clearly, this powerlessness will not be the end of the story. The truth will prevail among the helpless and strip the powerful who believe that they possess it by their power, or at least cure them of their deception. It is not as if the humiliated, insulted and outcast are already in possession of the truth simply because those who are powerful and sated are not; but they tend to think that they are a step nearer to it because they are not distracted from it by calculations of power and the need to preserve possessions. The sectarians Amos, Socrates, Jesus and Marx mentioned above each showed in his own way that powerlessness frees the mind rather than makes it stupid; that in the last instance suffering purifies more than it hardens; that generosity, compassion and solidarity achieve more than bitterness, stubbornness and envy. And no one who is still earnestly moved by the idea of an improvement in human conditions can completely cease to hope for it.

However, to speak for the powerless in this way is to expect great things of them. The general improvement is to start from them and infect all others, because under the pressure of their social situation they above all have the disposition for the better. However, the question is whether what their spokesmen hope of them is also what they themselves want. It is the same process as bringing up a family. A child of whom nothing is expected is not loved and has nothing to grow up to. By contrast, children and those who bring them up come to grief over excessive expectations. Correspondingly, intervention on behalf of the powerless and oppressed can be the first step to their liberation, but also to their subjection to expectations which are alien to them, towards unselfish surrender, and also towards a self-appointed leadership. And it is almost impossible to define precisely where the one begins and the other ends. Just try to put Jesus and Paul, Luther and Müntzer, Lenin and Luxemburg in one camp or the other!

No enlightened person likes to be told that all enlightenment and free-thinking has a sectarian root, from which indoctrination and fanaticism have sprouted abundantly, and thus are always in danger of taking on the features of these unattractive relatives. But it is no use: what is the wish of the post-moderns who are apparently so sorted out that they mock the blue-eyed nature of enlightenment human happiness? To enlighten their fellow men and women about an illusion in which they are trapped. In them, too, there is still a spark of that enthusiasm which wants to improve humankind: a denied retrogressive state of the sectarianism which they abhor.

The scope of this sectarianism is not to be underestimated. Its first historical manifestation is the preacher issuing a summons to repentance, who in the name of the deity by whom he feels chosen storms against a corrupt upper class which oppresses the people and leads them astray, and calls on the collective from which he has split off to return to the right way that he is depicting by the strict, mostly ascetic way of life which he requires of himself and his faithful followers. He represents the pre-critical form of the sectarian. He also regards the prevailing political power as untrue, and thus sees truth as a higher power which therefore is victorious in the last instance. Truth and power are already two things to him, but it is still inconceivable that the truth could have no power – that it could perish.

Where this notion dawns – and this happened first in modernity – sectarianism enters its critical phase. It then goes on to lose the certainty that it is under the protection of a higher power. Its cause can go wrong and simply depends on the recognition by as many people as possible who are suffering from existing circumstances that these circumstances are totally wrong. The preacher of repentance becomes a critical analyst. It is not enough to storm against the dominant power: its irrationality has to be demonstrated with irrefutable arguments. Truth extends as far as this demonstration succeeds and finds an echo. Here something 'higher', metaphysical, is no longer credited to a higher being, but accepted only to the degree that it has become something 'lower' and physical: an almost compulsive 'cannot do otherwise' than strive against the absurd disproportion between rational means and the irrational

overall structure of modern society which has taken
shape in flesh and blood.

However, even in this critical phase, where the call to
repent and be guided by God turned into the revolution
guided by reason, and its success for some decades
came into the sphere of the possible as a result of mass
readiness for it, even the most critical spirits found it
infinitely difficult no longer to appeal to something
higher. The feeling of being entrusted with the revelation of truth by favourable circumstances, though these
were called chance instead of God, and the longing for
this to be confirmed by something higher, whether the
dynamic of history or the pressure of the humiliated and
hurt for salvation, never completely left the thoughts
of people of the stature of Marx and Nietzsche,
Luxemburg and Benjamin. There is nothing disreputable about that, as long as the awareness of revelation and the need for confirmation does not snap and
come to depend on sayings of God and party decisions,
instead of being responsible to the only authority which
has any competence here: the uncensored use of reason.
A truth which does not want to be manifest and
confirmed is not the truth. Enlightenment which wants
to 'deconstruct' any claim to truth as untrue destroys
itself and helps to establish the post-critical phase of
sectarianism which, with the fall of the socialism of the
Eastern bloc, threatens to become the general state of
society.

The churches already practised this earlier, in the
1920s, when they joined together to form the ecumenical movement: not because of an attack of tolerance and
humanity, but because it was more advantageous for

them to co-operate than to work against one another in a world threatened by atheism. Nevertheless those who have difficulties with strange words, who notoriously confuse ecumenical and economical, are expressing a deep truth: just as competing firms in a business association organize their common interests, shelving those that divide them, so too do rival faith communities. Each is a sect to the others, but none may be given this name any longer. Only the clientele is presented with its own faith as still being the true faith. This topic is omitted from internal discussion. It is open only to those who do not belong to the inner group. Churches today tend to regard themselves as being rather different from sects. Their dignitaries warn about the dangers of fundamentalism with furrowed brows, as though their own teaching, which they derive from divine origins just as much as any Pentecostal preacher, were above any fundamentalism. But that is the sheer arrogance of power, which knows how to translate the privileges of past times into what matters today: market advantage. Where they clash, even those venerable religious communities which speak of others as a sectarian danger are not above reacting like any business in a crisis: they spend millions on advertising campaigns.

The ecumenical movement of the churches has long exercised what is now called communitarianism. What community one belongs to is secondary, provided that it is one which shows moral indignation: association, party, religious community. Their touchstone is the market of meaning. There they present their offer, which in each instance is as true as the investigation of it. That is how democracy works. Its scepticism about all unconditional truth does not notice how dogmatic it is. If no one can say with certainty what is true, then what the majority holds to be true is the truth. Anyone who has this on his side is right, and the greater the power of the media, the simpler it is. Thus in the post-critical phase of sectarianism, the separation of truth and power which had begun tenaciously in the pre-critical phase is gone back on with the most modern means.

Apocalypse

Many people believe that apocalypse means the end of the world: for them the word conjures up a vague picture of smoke, destruction, ruins and blood. But the Greek *apokalypsis* means revelation, and this is hardly associated with the end of the world any longer. That shows how far away we are from the thought of a time in which apocalypses were first written. They stem from the spiritual soil from which Christianity also emerged; they are works of desperation which went the rounds among the Jewish people from the second century before Christ, when its most precious heritage, which it had held in an iron grasp and cultivated through a history of centuries of suffering, threatened to slip away: the promise of the land of milk and honey.

Certainly people had swallowed the fact that the empirical Palestine, already at that time terrain which was being bitterly fought over, in which blood tended to flow rather than milk and honey, was not the Promised Land; but the notion on which the Jewish identity was orientated, namely that God would finally bring the history of its people, so full of deprivations, to an end in a state of peace and abundance, wherever this 'land' might be, had nevertheless remained. It remained until even the vain waiting and hope of generations began to crumble. What if history, which so far was making no move towards the Promised Land, was constructed in such a way that it did not even lead there? In that case the divine promise was humbug – unless history was on its way to an extreme point of catastrophe at which the world would be turned upside down: those on the bottom coming out on top, the inside becoming the outside, and the horror suffered by the just becoming their salvation.

Specifically apocalyptic writing begins with the imagination of such a turning-point in world history. It is the first theory of revolution. That the agents of this revolution could be other than God, his angels and hosts, still lies beyond its horizon. Human beings figure as its objects and at best are its conscious spectators: these are the apocalyptists. They interpret the current wars, famines and pestilences as a stage in a course of events which is constantly deteriorating, the prefigurements of greater abomination, and thus as heralds of that *katastrophe* (the literal translation of which is 'turning point') in which nature gets out of control and the dismay reaches a climax. 'Then the sun will suddenly appear by night and the moon by day. Blood will drip from trees and stones will cry out' (IV Ezra 5.4f.).

The notions that the apocalyptists have of the turmoil of the end time (almost all of them write pseudonymously, and adopt great old names like Moses, Isaiah, Daniel, etc.) are hardly less confusing than this confusion itself: fantasies of a decisive battle against the hosts of the evil one, and nature writhing in torment, overlap and intertwine – yet they have a clear basic notion in common: the worst terrors of this world form the birth pangs of a good new world. Where the horror is at its greatest, salvation is closest – at least for those who have not allowed themselves to be corrupted. At the moment when things come to a final climax, these people will be given a special *apokalypsis* (revelation) hidden from the great mass, so that they do not miss what the just are promised even in the last phase.

'Anyone who has a reason for living can bear almost anything,' we read in Nietzsche. The apocalypses are the desperate effort to preserve centuries of 'why?' and 'what for?' from collapse. Any everyday reflection and task has its little 'why?' and 'what for?'. It needs this, just as the body needs air to breathe. Human thought is notoriously and incurably orientated on a goal and a purpose, and Judaism developed its specific notion of salvation from this incurable fact. The little fleeting and everyday purposes in turn call for an overall purpose, a good end towards which history is moving and which it displays at specific moments. History is not always the same, but offers a chance to develop human forces to their optimum: this modern understanding of history as a process has its model in the notion of the Promised Land.

Apocalyptic provides the primal model for the challenge which arises for the whole idea of this process: what if the overall aim on which the lesser aims and purposes of everyday life are orientated dissolves? What if the way in which human thought and action is notoriously orientated on a goal and a purpose is not satisfied and justified by a good end, but simply runs on? In that case we have the crisis which the apocalyptists of antiquity attempted to avert by the notion of a world revolution – and which in modern times has become an epidemic which cannot be averted by any revolutionary efforts. Bourgeois society, which more than any previous society showed progress to be a force leading out of dependence and ignorance, has hardened into a process of devil take the hindmost. Its machinery runs just in order not to stand still, produces just for the sake of producing, and thus constantly increases its own destructive potential.

There are notions which show up the growth of human knowledge as untrue: but there are also those which it first *makes* true. That four is the number of the natural elements and one of them is the ground of all things was the most advanced state of knowledge among the pre-Socratics, and today is manifestly superstition. That the world is running towards its catastrophic end was a fantasy spinned by the apocalyptists and not supported by any scientific observation – and today it is truer than ever. Humankind has acquired the knowledge and ability to exterminate at least itself at a stroke. The problem is that to the degree that what they describe can actually be done, the old apocalyptic books lose their comforting meaning of revealing the plan of salvation which is hidden in all the distress. The Jewish apocalyptists could still say: what we are going through is still far from being the worst, and the worst will bring a change for the best, the world revolution brought about by God himself. But not even the boldest theologians venture to claim that the detonation of all available nuclear warheads could bomb in the new blessed world of the saved. Today's terrifying reports and images no longer have anything up their sleeve; it is ridiculous to see God's hint, the birthpangs of God's kingdom, in them when we know that they are an integral element of the everyday products of industry. The apocalypse no longer reveals anything higher; it is reduced to a vision of sheer horror (often televised) – and the inability to cope with it rationally.

Günther Anders has called this inability 'apocalypse blindness'. 'Through our technology we have got into a situation in which we can no longer imagine what we can produce and what we can do.' 'Even twenty dead say no more to us, at least to our feelings, than ten dead.' 'But the soul goes on strike against the thought of the apocalypse. The thought remains a word.'[21] Individual feeling is far from being able to cope with the real extent of the terror any longer. We have no sense of the danger, which only makes it more dangerous, and no one can make those few light moments in which we are less terrified about the danger itself than about our disproportionate emotional relationship to it last. Anders' discoveries appeared four decades ago, and the *Limits of Growth* report of the Club of Rome two decades ago; the cry that it was five to midnight swelled to a chorus of people giving warnings and admonitions. Yet it made no lasting impression on humankind unless this was subcutaneous, in that two apparently opposed strategies of immunization were developed.

One strategy, which is 'higher', presents itself as a reflection above all sensationalism and panic-mongering; it gives the impression that apart from an insignificant remnant of risk everything is under control, or turns up its nose at the 'apocalyptic tone in philosophy which has recently arisen' (thus Derrida), which fails to note that the problem of the apocalypse has 'always existed'. The other strategy, which is 'lower', is a kind of flight forward: a greed for horror scenes. News broadcasts and feature films in which none appear are increasingly felt to be like soup without salt: insipid. Gone are the times when the aura of the beautiful and the illusory world of advertising were the main means of bewitchment against unadorned reality. People increasingly inoculate themselves against its terrors by the consumption of audio-visual horror in which one experiences everything and yet comes out of it with a 'healthy goose pimples', as Ulrich Horstmann puts it.

To the degree that only something like this still captivates people, is felt to be authentic and living, we can see how little our contemporaries still perceive their life as their own and as authentic life. The greed for audio-visual apocalypses teaches us how far life is experienced as a time of dispossession. Horror scenes become fulfilled moments of an empty time; they appear less as what can be in store for one than as what momentarily saves one from the horror of emptiness, a horror which passes with a typical motion of the hand reaching for the on-off switch. This horror is a nightmare which increases to the degree that the feelings become deaf to the really great terrifying events: it has no smell or image; it has nothing that one can hold on to, that one could name, from which one could distance oneself. It is not to be confused with the good old boredom meant by Schopenhauer, which gapes in a state of satisfaction and inactivity, but interposes itself in any second which is not filled with background music, television or being busy. Those same contemporaries who placidly cook their steaks to pictures from Rwanda get restless when their television sets break down or the background music stops. Their hunger to have horror around them is an attempt to ward off a horror which clings closer and tighter than any shirt. Their greed for apocalypse is the most progressive form of their blindness to apocalypse.

There is no point in wanting to stir them out of this with new, stronger doses of horror. At best they can come to reflect at that point where, hard-boiled though they are to all audio-visual impacts, they are as sensitive as the princess to the pea: where the horror of the void threatens to mount. Nietzsche's 'anyone who has a reason for living can bear almost anything' was not primarily directed against this. He was thinking primarily of the dumb religious beast to the slaughter, prepared for and also capable of enormous sacrifices and deprivation as long as it takes its god or idols as valid currency. But to the degree that such a 'Why?' which holds together body and soul disintegrates, not only the readiness but also the capacity for privation disappears – and the religious beast for the slaughter in retrospect proves to be cunning. It knew how to exploit the spiritual force of the 'Why?', it suspected that anyone who no longer has any reason for living can no longer bear almost any form of life either. The result is that modern social character who does not want to go without anything, does not want to put himself out for anything, because he does not see why, and for whom even the most remarkable ideas, deeds, experiences are devalued so that they become banalities, because he can no longer sense what these could be good for. His life becomes empty, however full his diary may be, and not to suffer this emptiness is the incessant effort of the organization of his body and soul. Here we have that omnipresent and incomprehensible permanent stress which poses so many riddles to doctors and psychologists, and which represents the microcosm of the apocalyptic horror that is experienced every day, whereas the macrocosm as depicted in audio-visual form no longer seriously affects anyone.

There is no doubt that modern society *is* apocalyptic, not only in the sense that at every moment the Damoclean sword of apocalyptic annihilation hangs over it, but also because if it continues, in the long term it will allow only one choice: that between fundamentalism and nihilism. And the option for the former will less and less become an intellectual decision. It will be a necessity for psychological hygiene: either one clings to some higher reason – even if it can barely withstand rational examination for a moment – in order to keep viable or competent, or one falls victim to the loss of perspective of a society which is going nowhere, arouses no more expectations, and makes not only any deprivation but even the normal everyday greyness intolerable. The hypersensitivity of the unfeeling is the psychological and physical characteristic of the apocalyptic state.

No one can identify a way out of it any longer. No one dares to mention even in a whisper the cure which the ancient apocalyptists thought they knew in their theological exuberance: world revolution. In principle this, too, like collective destruction, has become a human possibility in modern times. However, here possibility and reality fall apart to a degree which cannot be bridged. Pressing a couple of buttons could bring about destruction. World revolution calls for overcoming the self to join in a global mass action, to which nothing points and for which everything speaks. If the present catastrophes are not the birth pangs of deliverance, they are nevertheless an imperative to revolution. This imperative is as impotent as it is categorical, and it is no more falsified by falling on deaf ears than is the rhyme, 'All the wheels must now stand still, if that is thy mighty will'.

For one thing is certain: the apocalyptic state will last at least as long as the modern commodity-producing society whose mechanisms of market and competition which have produced it with intrinsic consistency. The present world may not claim to be the best of all possible worlds. But if it appears as a world without any alternative, then is it not *as good as the best*, following the motto, 'These trousers may not be my best, but they are my only ones'? The very fact that the view that the existing shape of society, its technological and cultural achievements, cry out for another use than that to which they are being put is quite naturally regarded as being less absurd than a revolution in its basic capitalist structure speaks volumes. It is due to the most simplistic idolization of power: what rules has authority; what does not become anything is worthless – forget it. As long as this forgetting has the upper hand, there is nothing to be done about the blindness to apocalypse.

Reconciliation

Heinrich and Thomas Mann fell out and finally became reconciled. As the last Russian troops left, they sang 'Germany, we stretch out our hands to you', and the leading articles praised the reconciliation which had now taken the place of the occupation. Being reconciled means settling a dispute, arriving at a peaceful agreement: between individuals, groups or whole peoples.

One stage further, and the term takes on a cosmic theological dimension. God 'reconciled the cosmos to himself in Christ' (II Cor. 5.19), asserts the apostle Paul, by which he means that the rift which has run through nature since the Fall and makes 'the whole creation groan in travail together until now' (Rom. 8.22) has now been healed – that rift which opened up with eating from the tree of knowledge: through the rise of the human intellect from nature. The intellect is to blame for the rift, and its action does not restore it.

Therefore, according to the apostle, God has personally anticipated the healing of it in the figure of his Son and promised this healing to all those who understand it as such. However, Paul wavers: was the anticipated reconciliation already everything, and only needs to be tried for right disposition and good behaviour to be rewarded abundantly on the the last day? Or was it a 'reckoning' (II Cor. 5.5) – the introduction of a work of reconciliation to be done by human beings, constantly narrowing the cosmic rift so that the last day will only dot the 'i' of the consummation which is reserved for God? Down to the present day the whole theological dispute over reconciliation vacillates between these two versions: if reconciliation is still to come, what *is* it then? A fulfilled reality which does not exist or a promise which is not being fulfilled? In both cases it is an unlaid egg, and theology is the scholarly enterprise to prove that it has been laid.

Theologians often interpret their terms in the same way as artists interpret their works: badly. So let us take a step back to the setting where the concept of reconciliation is really at home: in the market place. The peaceful agreement denoted by the Greek *katallage* is primarily that of exchange. Coming to an agreement with others instead of robbing them, offering them appropriate recompense for the commodity that one would like to have from them, is one of the greatest cultural achievements. A settlement does not function without understanding and agreement; it buries the hatchet and allows peace to begin.

That one senses so little of this in our modern commercial society is because of its other side. Because everyone trades to his own advantage, the danger of going too far is inherent in any trading. Anyone who trades has to make sure that he does not come off badly, that nothing of unequal value is traded to his disadvantage. So trade is also the sphere of the suspicious examination, the look which measures and weighs up;

it is the sphere of rationalized and domesticated hostility. Its whole scope becomes evident where those who trade are not putting *something* on offer but trading *themselves*, because that is the only way in which they can survive. Their persons and labour are now just as much the object of the calculating assessment as a pair of shoes or a head of cattle, and if they are done down because they are forced to sell themselves, this is not only bad business but an act which determines their whole social status. In this way domination and exploitation are sealed by contract in modern society – and denied, as they do not take place without the agreement of those who are dominated and exploited. These are not brought in handcuffs to sign their contracts of employment.

Trading works at two levels: justice and peaceful compensation are its surface, and hostility, doing down and domination are its under side. Trading promises far more than it offers. Not that it offers nothing at all: every notion of justice is orientated on a trade-off, but that does not mean the strict recompense of like with like is always just. No reconciliation can take place without a peaceful balancing of various claims, but such a balance is not yet the whole of reconciliation. And when Paul gave the twilight market term *katallage* a theological loading, he had all this in mind: a peaceful settlement without calculation and disadvantage by the standards of the world – so that the sighing of creation might cease.

Paul was already aware that earthly beings will not be in a position to achieve this, and from it he drew the bold conclusion: only God can do this – and has already done it. 'In itself' the rift in nature, alias our guilt, has already been blotted out. And are we so damaged by it that we hardly notice? This very scandal sets in motion that pressure to justify God which is called theology, and which finds a thousand good reasons in human failure and the divine plan of salvation to explain why the world after Christ is not a jot better than it was before.

A knowingness about what cannot be known which presents itself in the humility of faith is at work here. It already begins where people believe that they know that the world is 'creation': made by a God who wants only the best so to speak as his blessed sounding-board, which is then silenced by the rift made in it through the fall of human beings. Here God himself is also stuck in the mire. If he does not want to allow the human corruption of his creation to triumph over his good intentions, i.e. if he does not want to resign, he is himself compelled to perform the reconciliation which human beings are not achieving – and make them repent for it: he promises them a reconciliation the enjoyment of which he postpones for the foreseeable future.

That is the unnamed subtext of the reciprocal resentment that goes with the often-told myth of the divine act of reconciliation, as the underside goes with the surface. The notion of reconciliation has been bedevilled by the spell of this myth: reconciliation has been got round by the opposite of what it really means. The corset of God's compulsory justification robs him of his own theological breath. He can only draw this breath when he is detached from the untenable certainty of a course of the world runs between paradise and bliss. Its truth-content can develop only when it becomes clear that it is nothing but an idea: its full realization does not lie within the realm of human possibilities and has no supernatural guarantees, yet nevertheless is an indispensable focal point for all thought and action.

The notion of reconciliation has something that one might least expect from a theological concept: the structure of fulfilled human reason projected on to a cosmic dimension. To think rationally entails interweaving concepts, judgments, conclusions coherently, without any blunders slipping in here and there. The avoidance of contradiction is the basic law of the intellect and applies not only inwardly, to its logical operations, but also outwardly, to its relationship to the physical world. For even a crazy system can have an intrinsically logic construction – starting from an untenable presupposition like that the dice is round or that all the world is persecuting me.

Ideas must have some support in the things with which they deal, if they are to be more than fantasies. The correspondence between the intellect and the things that it claims to express is therefore an old criterion for truth which is indispensable, yet can never be wholly fulfilled. For what does correspondence mean? Ideas never reproduce things as they are, but always in an abstract, faded, schematized form. How many thousands of properties and characteristics must so simple a concept as a tree omit in order to be capable of covering the great variety of different trees? The agreement between concept and thing is never complete; yet the 'drive' of reason, its inner regularity which compels it to avoid contradiction, would be satisfied only by a complete accord with the totality of the world in which it finds itself. The drive to avoid contradiction means far more than the compulsion towards correct logical operations. It contains a longing for the healing of the 'rift' which is in fact in the world, since there is such a thing as intellect, which ensures that its abstract schemes do not manage to coincide with concrete things; that it is not in accord with the physical drives on which it is imposed and the organism in which it dwells and is not fused into an integral, indestructible unity. That is why decay, sickness and death are experiences with which it cannot cease to dispute, even if it says that they are 'quite natural'.

But this wrangling betrays the fact that the longing for the abolition of misery and death is actually part of that abolition. It expresses in thought what the 'sighing of the creation' says without concepts and yet unmistakably: it will cease. 'Woe says, Begone! But joy would have eternity', and this longing, translated into logic, means that every contradiction will cease. In the rare moments of pleasure, the surrender to a person, thing or idea in which one forgets oneself, there flashes out something of that reconciliation of intellect and nature which, if it lasted, would be what theology calls eternal bliss.

The self-enlightenment of the human intellect includes the discovery that it has an incurable theological bent: it can ignore the longing for reconciliation, but it will not get rid of it. That bent is there even in its simplest logical activities. It cannot but investigate, explain, interpret, i.e. bring unity to multiplicity; connection, order and meaning to what is disparate. Its action wills the world to be *whole*.

Reconciliation

Neither modern unbelievers nor modern believers want to know about this theological infection of the human reason. They are pragmatists in reconciliation, agreed in the calculation: what use to us is an idea of reconciliation that cannot be realized? None at all. So, one side concludes, there must be a supernatural reconciler of the world – and they fall into the trap of the theological compulsion to justify. So, the others conclude, let us dispense with the reconciliation of the world and content ourselves with what can be done, like settling disputes wherever they arise and guaranteeing democratic conditions in which human beings can attain to unforced understanding and agreement. And if that happened, that would be a very great deal.

But what does 'unforced' mean? There is no consistent concept of an absence of compulsion and a freedom from violence which would not coincide with the theological concept of reconciliation. Any agreement in communication, any co-operation in solidarity which the present conditions of life allow, has traces of the distress, violation, force which it has outgrown. Communication free of domination would have to be what the theologians call *communicatio idiomatum*: a reciprocal communication of properties, in other words an exchange deepened to the point of becoming reciprocal surrender and permeation: reconciliation. But anyone who only strives for conditions which are 'approximately' free from violence and domination is either also thinking of *what* they approximate to, namely the reconciled state, or his thought is nonsensical: a freedom from violence and domination achieved through a lack of reconciliation.

What Price Religion?

The idea of reconciliation is a kind of star of Bethlehem for reason. It cannot be grasped, but it tells reason where it is to go and points the way there with a power which is noticeable above all when it ceases to shine. That point marks the beginning of a superficiality which no longer sees any settlement and agreement between human beings against its un-named background and support, but already takes any reciprocity to be fairness and justice, any compromise to be an act of reconciliation, any democratic form of trading to be non-violent. It is as though violence only began when fists and weapons were used and not already in the universal compulsory exchange that constitutes modern society; as though democracy were already a good thing in itself and not also the most progressive form possible of administrating the misery of the world. No wonder that the discussion about social theory in our time, the 'methodological atheism' which knows nothing higher than categories of the market and democracy, works on disseminating and making scientific that twilight which is disseminated by trade and which Paul at any rate began to dissipate a bit when he deepened the market term *katallage* so that it became a theological concept.

In all this, it is as though there were a secret conspiracy between atheism and theism. Much as they are opposed to each another, they are unanimous in seeing only two possibilities: either one believes in higher beings or one does not; one is religious or one is not. That is the picture of the world which both maintain, and much more irritating to both than the position of the opposite side is the notion that this picture of the world cannot be right. Anyone who says that religion itself ruins its central concepts, whereas the areligious carry around far more of its fragments undigested than they notice, and that neither does what is really important, namely to rescue the damaged intellect here, gets on the nerves of both sides. They feel that he is meddling in their internal concerns, which, as it is so beautifully put, 'everyone must work out for himself', whether he believes or not. But it is high time to get involved here. The dualistic view of the world which divides human beings into the religious and the non-religious, like smokers and non-smokers, never had less to do with reality than today. Its fall is long overdue.

Postscript

Anyone who writes a series gets letters from readers, and if he has made it his task to demonstrate the inappropriateness of the dualistic picture of the world which divides human beings into religious and non-religious, he is certain of incurring the disquiet of those who cling to this picture. Such people fall into three categories.

First come the theists. If for a start we leave aside the hard-liners who hurl biblical quotations like thunder-bolts and because of my errors commend me to Christian prayer ('According to God's Word he is a blind man, paralysed – like the wretched people to whom Jesus always came first'), there remain those who are open to the world, who with a gesture of superiority accuse anyone who does not talk about the content of faith in the language of faith of failing to understand. Why was a philosopher allowed to write this series instead of a theologian, who would really have under-stood about these things? The author is also said to be emotionally incompetent ('He has little inkling of religion. The view that distress and violence are the breeding ground for religious feeling shows how far what the writer regards as religion is from what it

94

really is'), nor up to date with scholarship: 'Do we have to analyse once again what it is to believe? To repeat once again that it is "neither a rational proof nor an irrational feeling nor a decision of the will but a well-founded trust which in this sense is also completely rational" and includes "thinking, questioning and doubt, and at the same time is a matter of the understanding, the will and the disposition"' (Hans Küng in *Credo*)?

Indeed, with such formulations they have been cheating for decades, these modern enlightened theologians who are so infinitely interested in critical thought. Their motto is: 'Anyone who has not felt it will not get it.' This is the accusation they make against the Vatican when it requires obedience to dogma from them. Dogmas, they argue, are merely the time-conditioned linguistic version of an unconditional experience of God which precedes all language. For anyone who does not have this, dogmatic formulae are merely dead letters and tinkling cymbals; but anyone who has it is not only free but also obliged to express it today in accordance with his time, just as the church of the fourth Christian century did in its, and that means in a modern way, including all questions and doubt.

Neither dogma nor the criticism of religion are said to come anywhere near the direct experience of God that is claimed. The same motto, 'Anyone who does not feel it cannot have a say', applies to it, and where the criticism of religion has a say it is always already talking about dogmatic formulae. It is talking to the wrong people if it confuses these formulae with living faith; it is cherishing an antiquated 'picture of God coloured in the style of the Nazarene' if it calls for a proof for the existence of God, and theology which is up to date has got far beyond this. Prove God? That would mean unworthily to make the one who is beyond our control an object under human control and to force him into logical categories which he explodes. Only those who feel it will get it. In other words, faith is not an objectivizing approach which holds things to be true, but a holistic affirmation which embraces all dimensions and abysses of human existence. Well said, but the basis of the statement is that the proof for God which is declared impossible and unnecessary has already succeeded: that the one who is beyond our control and is totally affirmed also actually exists. Otherwise the whole affirmation would be about nothing.

Moreover the allegedly direct experience of God is never pure experience, but always already experience plus a conclusion which is not backed by any experience. That when one feels inwardly moved one has not been overwhelmed, say, by one's own feelings and notions, but by the Most High himself, is neither felt nor experienced, but merely concluded. At the crucial point we find the surreptitious conclusion from feelings, notions and concepts to the existence of a being who corresponds to these feelings, notions and concepts: a bare logical operation, namely that of the conclusion – and an inappropriate one at that. And so as not to show up its nakedness – the classical proofs of God at least played their cards openly and worked with all the achievements of human acumen – there is the swindle of being existentially or totally moved. This attitude is in reality indebted to a proof of God which it condescendingly counts as part of yesterday's world.

Postscript

A faith which seeks to immunize itself with secret and smart rational conclusions is truly not as honest as it seems. It proves itself all the more to be what the atheists claim to have known long since. If God does not exist, all searching for the grain of truth in the chaff of religion is useless, and those who cannot stop doing this belong among those half-hearted people who simply cannot consistently detach themselves from its magic.

Moreover this suspicion of my series is also nurtured by those on the other side of the dualistic picture of the world, the atheists. Some of them, for example, read an 'argument in favour of the blasphemy paragraph' out of the article on blasphemy, which was said to show 'how simply even today one can still issue the call to censorship'. Perception can really be so distorted only where mere intellectual contact with themes like contempt for religion, God, meaning, are compulsively and painfully associated with the clergy, the church, and all that they drum into a person. In this atheistic over-sensitivity there is anxiety about the proof of God – not that it could fail, which would still allow it to potter around under the cloak of self-denial, but that it could well succeed, so that as with the evil spirit, a mere mention of the name will summon the one named to come in person to get the one who spoke it.

This kind of anxiety about the proof of God is, of course, anxiety about the empty spaces, the wounds, that the non-existence of God leaves behind. Anything formed by human feelings or thoughts twines around persons, events, circumstances which give it firmness, support, shape. These things form the realm of higher

97

powers – whether one calls them gods or something else is a terminological question, which no adolescent individual can fail to go by or identify with. There is no such thing as a strictly areligious childhood without faith, and atheism is effective only to the degree that one becomes detached from one's own childhood – and that is never complete. Moreover, as surely as one learns that things have causes and modes of behaviour have grounds, so gradually the question of a first cause, a first ground, becomes pressing. Conversely, the fact that one sets aims unavoidably produces the notion of a final aim without which all everyday aims are left hanging, with no meaning or purpose. However much human beings enlighten themselves and unmask the higher powers of their childhood as spectres, as long as they are beings with needs they will not get rid of the need for a first ground and an ultimate purpose, an origin and destiny of their insecure existence to support and protect them. That means that they also will not get rid of the temptation to invent a higher being who is well disposed towards them to play this role. If they resist this temptation, it immediately looks for another home: the existence of such a being also brings the need to deny him – as though in this way one could become as autonomous, exalted, unshakeable – in a word as adult – as Epicurus makes the wise man or Nietzsche the superman. Theism invents God, and atheism a human being who does not need him. Now the existing possibilities of mitigating human need are scandalously unexhausted. But this need would cease completely only in a state of eternal bliss, and only a God could produce that. In the last resort human need is a need for God, and the idea of God is therefore an inexpressible element of human beings' unconstrained reflection on themselves – even if God does not exist.

Hardly anyone dares to dispute publicly that God is not particularly suitable as a theme for multiple choice, where one puts a cross against Yes, No, Don't Know. It is all the more illuminating that in almost all attitudes towards the topic, if we take away the verbosity and learning, this framework, which is said to be far too primitive, remains. The dualistic view of the world knows believers, unbelievers and a third kind: the indifferent, who find my series superfluous because it deals with questions of faith which each individual must sort out for himself, and therefore unnecessarily intimidates people instead of contributing to the clarification of some relevant problem. Whether such people think it does not matter whether or not one believes in God, or regard such belief as a highly respectable decision by someone which is not to be interfered with, they share a dualistic world with all those who regard themselves as believers or unbelievers. Even among the circle of those who have followed this series and its attempt to break through the rigidity of dualism with feelings ranging from interest to approval, there are those who ask what I end up with after all the turns that my argument takes. Am I a believer or an unbeliever, and why do I keep prevaricating? My answer is that I am not prevaricating. I do not have an unwritten secret teaching behind what I have written like Plato, but believe what I say and write openly: that we can no longer deal with modern reality by means of the concepts of belief and unbelief, and that those who confess one or the other do not know what they are doing. Theism today is itself deeply permeated with unbelief, and atheism is far from being as unbelieving as it pretends to be. An account has to be given of how each permeates the other, and neither of them is any longer what it pretends to be.

'A treasure lies in our vineyard,' says the dying father in Bürger's poem, and after his death his sons immediately go out and plough up the vineyard, turning over the soil. They do not find the treasure, but thanks to this work they get such an abundant harvest that they finally realize what the treasure really consists of. This poem has not only an economic but also a theological sense. Religion does not hide the divine treasure which it promises. But ploughing through and turning over its thoughts can help it to a fertility for which the present still largely lacks sense organs.

Notes

1. Quoted from K. Hammer, *Deutsche Kriegstheologie*, Munich 1974, 318f.
2. M. Luther, 'On The Jews and Their Lies', *Luther's Works* 47, 275.
3. Cf. G. Mensching (ed.), *Das Testament des Abbé Meslier*, Frankfurt am Main 1976.
4. Marquis de Sade, *Philosophy in the Boudoir*, London 1991, 155.
5. R. Webster, *A Brief History of Blasphemy: Liberalism, Censorship and the Satanic 'Verses'*, London 1990.
6. F. Nietzsche, *Beyond Good and Evil*, 25.
7. F. Nietzsche, *The Joyful Wisdom*, 1886 preface.
8. Ignatius, *To the Romans*, 5.2.
9. Mensching (ed.), *Testament des Abbé Meslier* (n.3), 85.
10. W. Benjamin, *Franz Kafka. Zur zehnten Wiederkehr seines Todestages, Gesammelte Schriften*, ed. Tiedemann and Schweppenhäuser, II, 2, Frankfurt am Main 1977, 412.
11. I. Kant, *Religion within the Limits of Reason Alone*, reissued New York 1960, 182–3.
12. F. Nietzsche, *Thus Spoke Zarathustra*, IV. The Drunken Song, 12.
13. M. Weber, 'Politik als Beruf', in id., *Gesammelte Politische Schriften*, Tübingen ⁵1988, 508.
14. F. Nietzsche, *Twilight of the Idols*.

What Price Religion?

15. Augustine, *Confessions* X, 6.
16. E. Reuter, 'Wie schafft bessere Erkenntnis besseres Handeln', *Frankfurter Rundschau*, 2 July 1993, documentation.
17. S. Freud, 'A Seventeenth-Century Demonological Neurosis' (1923), in *Collected Works* 14, Harmondsworth 1985, 377–424.
18. H. Haag, *Abschied vom Teufel*, Einsiedeln 1969, 10.
19. Nietzsche, *Beyond Good and Evil* (n.6), 26.
20. F. Nietzsche, *Ecce Homo*, 'Thus Spoke Zarathustra', 3.
21. G. Anders, *Die atomare Drohung*, Munich ⁵1986, 73; id., *Die Antiquiertheit des Menschen* I, Munich 1956, 269.